THE
Landscape
Makeover
BOOK

How to Bring New Life
to an Old Yard

THE
Landscape
Makeover
BOOK

Sara Jane von Trapp

The Taunton Press

Publisher: Jim Childs

Editors: Cherilyn DeVries, Cheryl Winters-Tetreau

Editorial Assistants: Meredith DeSousa, Susan Ferrelli

Copy Editor: Cathleen Reinfelder

Designers: Henry Roth, Stephen Hughes

Layout Artists: Henry Roth, Lori Wendin

Front cover photographers: Dency Kane (center); © Alan and Linda Detrick (top right); Boyd Hagan, © The Taunton Press, Inc. (center right); Susan Kahn, © The Taunton Press, Inc. (bottom right); J. Paul Moore (bottom left)

Back cover photographers: Delilah Smittle, © The Taunton Press, Inc. (top); Boyd Hagan, © The Taunton Press, Inc. (bottom left); Judi Rutz, © The Taunton Press, Inc. (bottom right)

Photographer p. ii and 2: J. Paul Moore

Photographers p. vi (top to bottom): Janet Loughrey, Scott Gibson, © Alan and Linda Detrick, © Alan and Linda Detrick, © Alan and Linda Detrick

Photographers p. 1 (top to bottom): Steve Silk, © The Taunton Press, Inc.; Charles Miller, © The Taunton Press, Inc.; Delilah Smittle, © The Taunton Press, Inc.; Marvin Sloben, © The Taunton Press, Inc.; Boyd Hagan, © The Taunton Press, Inc.

Illustrator: Scott Bricher

Indexer: Nancy Bloomer

Taunton
BOOKS & VIDEOS
for fellow enthusiasts

Text © 2000 by Sara Jane von Trapp
Illustrations © 2000 by The Taunton Press, Inc.

Printed in the United States of America
10 9 8 7 6 5 4 3 2 1

The Taunton Press, Inc., 63 South Main Street, PO Box 5506, Newtown, CT 06470-5506
e-mail: tp@taunton.com

Distributed by Publishers Group West

Library of Congress Cataloging-in-Publication Data
von Trapp, Sara Jane.
    The landscape makeover book : how to bring new life to an old yard / Sara Jane von Trapp.
        p. cm.
    ISBN 1-56158-259-X
    1. Landscape gardening. 2. Landscape architecture. I. Title.
SB473.V665   2000
635.9—dc21   99-053375

Acknowledgments

I particularly wish to acknowledge the patience and toiling of my husband, Tom Goelz. He suffered through the disarray of a torn-up yard as well as the soreness from digging holes for plants. He took my planting directions gracefully even though I knew he was not too happy about it. For every hole I asked him to dig, he found huge roots and huge rocks, but he persevered. Most of all, he joins me often on the deck or in the yard to survey our domain, and he delights in my delight at the results of our labor.

To our six children, Kate, Jake, Becca, Charlie, Bobby, and Margi, who seem to get as much satisfaction from the beauty and fun environment we have created as we do.

Many people and businesses helped make this book happen. Not every task went smoothly, but the result was worth the effort and frustration. First, I'd like to thank Helen Albert of The Taunton Press for her involvement early on, and several editors along the way including Cherilyn DeVries, Susan Ferelli, and Cheryl Winters-Tetreau, who worked on the majority of the book. Cheryl picked up the pieces and made it happen. Thanks to photographer Boyd Hagen, who spent many days traipsing around Connecticut with me to capture most of the images in this book and to his predecessor, Sloan Howard, who spent many hours as well. Thanks to illustrator Scott Bricher, who worked magic with my lousy art scraps.

The following companies, all here in Connecticut, went out of their way to meet deadlines and contribute to the landscape renovation of 48 Meeker Hill: Connecticut Arborists, Inc. of Monroe; Connecticut Landscapes of Easton; L & J Pool of Bethel; Mason Medic, Inc. of Bethel; our carpenter, Richard Kaechele, of Bethel; Steck's Nursery of Bethel; and Walpole Woodworkers of Ridgefield.

Thanks to Twombly Nursery of Monroe, Connecticut, for providing personnel and their nursery for several location photos.

A special thanks to Alan Lafer and Susan Rose, who let me borrow their beautiful property for parts of this project, and to their landscaper, Antonio Albanese of Bedford Hills, New York, and his crew for their hard work and cooperation.

And, finally, there are several images in this book that aren't so beautiful. We photographed many features in the landscape that were in need of renovation in order to articulate the need for the book. It is those homeowners and those properties for whom this book is written, and I hope that you will forgive me for making examples of your foibles. I hope you will understand that because of your contributions to this book, many homeowners will benefit.

Contents

Introduction

Landscape renovation can be a daunting task. You've inherited someone else's 30-year-old yard, and you don't know where to begin. The walkway to the front door is barely visible as the plants and lawn vie for the same space. Or maybe you did the landscaping 30 years ago and the house has slowly disappeared behind a jungle of plants. The patio never really seemed big enough and now with the grandchildren visiting, it doesn't work at all.

This book will help you see the trees in that forest and give your home and yard new life. Instead of ripping it all out and starting over, you should assess what you have and decide what is worth keeping. Once you consider the lay of the land and take an objective view of the neighborhood, you can redefine the yard.

The next step is to take a hard look at your plants and follow a checklist of makeover strategies. Which ones do you trash and which ones do you prune and give new shape? Because some of those older varieties of plants have been replaced by new cultivars chosen for compactness, improved color, and insect and disease resistance, you'll learn how to transplant them to other areas of the yard or move them around in the planting bed to better utilize their assets. I'll guide you in choosing new companion plants and in redesigning the landscape, integrating the new with the old.

The most important part of your yard is the front entry. I'll help you transform a tired walkway and front stoop with makeover tricks of the trade. In the backyard, you can enlarge and reshape the outdoor living space and even renew the existing patio with fresh materials. You can add that swimming pool you've always wanted, but didn't know where to build, or construct a garden pool and let the fish do the swimming! Lighting is the final touch, and one that enhances all your hard work, along with safely guiding you and your guests from one end of the yard to the other. And the latest lighting systems are easy to design, install, and use.

Like adding a coat of paint or a new carpet to the living room, a landscape facelift will invigorate the yard, add value to your home, and give you a new outlook. So put on your gardening gloves and get out the pruning shears: It's time to begin your landscape makeover.

1 House and Garden Style: From Young to Old to Rejuvenated

Landscaping is a scary, overwhelming endeavor for most people. In over 20 years of designing, installing, and consulting with homeowners about their landscaping, I have found few people confident enough to tackle the project without help. Trepidation is understandable when you are starting from scratch, but landscaping seems to be even more overwhelming when you have an old, overgrown yard and no idea where to start.

Renovating an existing landscape can be a daunting task, but the results are well worth the trouble. (Photo by Janet Loughrey.)

It's very likely that your yard's ready-for-renovation design belongs to what could be called the American Style of Landscaping. You know the look: tall, overgrown evergreens on either side of the front door; lower (but still overgrown) evergreens clinging to the foundation and arranged in a straight line to follow the walls of the house. This "style" was created by default over the past century as homeowners did everything they could to hide foundations and clothe their homes in plantings. Without regard to house and garden style, the same design traveled from house to house, neighborhood to neighborhood, all around the country. Unfortunately, this style is still commonly used today. In this book, I will give you creative strategies for replacing this style or other boring, overgrown landscapes with one that suits your home and lifestyle.

Where Do I Begin?

Any landscaping design can be transformed from an overgrown jungle to an attractive setting for your home. If you take your yard sector by sector and element by element and break the project down into a series of steps, I guarantee you will find the job less intimi-

This overgrown yard desperately needs a fix-up. Plantings are threatening to cover the windows, and the monocolor is uninteresting. (Photo courtesy *Fine Gardening* magazine; © The Taunton Press, Inc.)

dating. To build a house, you start with a plan and then begin building from the foundation up. With renovation, the process is just the opposite. You dissect the elements from the top down and then make a plan for rebuilding the landscape. The plan will incorporate the good parts of your old landscaping with your new ideas for the yard. If you don't have new ideas now, they will come as you break down the existing spaces.

START WITH SECTORS

The first step is to divide your entire property into sectors: the front yard, backyard, right side yard, left side yard, and perimeters. If you have additional areas on the property, such as a pool area or woods, you should add those sectors to your evaluation. Look at each sector individually during your evaluation, but be aware that sectors may overlap. For instance, when you look at the front yard, keep the side yards in the back of your mind because plantings may tie together or walkways may lead from the front to the back through the sides. Alternatively, when you look at the backyard, the perimeters will be important to examine for shade and privacy. The three main areas to evaluate in each sector of your yard are the plantings, the hardscape, and the whole picture of the yard and lawn.

An aesthetically pleasing yard makes you feel good, and part of feeling good is the pride you take in making your yard a showpiece for friends. But as you examine the various parts of your yard, you are also evaluating them for how they fit your family's needs and lifestyle. The examination goes beyond aesthetics and beauty. For instance, you may know your patio is made of mundane concrete and has cracks in it, but your family's needs for the patio also say it is not big enough or the right shape. It is important to make your yard comfortable and usable for your family as well as beautiful.

As you evaluate the sectors of your yard, keep track of your impressions in a diary or journal. This will give you a more intimate and subjective view of the strengths and areas for improvement. After you evaluate your yard, you'll be looking at the neighborhood and at individual plantings in your landscape. Keep your diary handy as you continue to explore these elements. You will use it to identify your old plants, to decide what to keep and move, and to determine what, if any, new plants you will add to the beds. As you read this book, you will use your diary over and over to help you formulate a plan and a timeline for getting the tasks done.

EXAMINE THE PLANTINGS

Take a look at your plants and where they are planted. Generally speaking, plants are the easiest part of a landscape to change, and they are key to enhancing your yard and house. The following questions will help you determine which plants in each sector need the most attention. Jot down your answers in your diary.

- Are the plantings healthy looking or do they look like they're dead or dying? Are they overgrown or diseased or full of insects? If they are flowering plants, do they flower well?
- Are the planting beds crowded? Straight lined with plants? Do the plants look like they're crammed against the house? Are the planting beds wide enough?
- Are windows blocked by overgrown plants?
- Are the plants near the foundation as tall as the front facade of the house?
- Is the planting boring or colorful? Is there a mix of evergreen and deciduous? Woody and herbaceous?
- Do the plants offer enough color and interest throughout the seasons? Which season(s) are more drab?

Well-maintained backyard plantings have a neat, manicured appearance. Serpentine beds and deep edging look professionally done, but it's easy to achieve this look yourself. (Photo © Alan and Linda Detrick.)

Color and unique shapes highlight this foundation planting with a vine and topiary spiral. Note that while the plantings are asymmetrical, they are also balanced, and plants are kept below or at windowsill height. (Photo by Maureen Gilmer.)

- Is any foundation showing where it shouldn't be?
- Do the trees near the house offer enough shade or too much?
- Do the plants I want to keep need more than a few hours per week of my time to maintain? If yes, do I have the time to dedicate to a high-maintenance landscape?

EVALUATE THE HARDSCAPING

Hardscaping includes anything in the yard that isn't alive, from sidewalks to fences. Changing a hardscaping element usually requires more labor and expense, but it's a long-term investment. As you look at the hardscaping in each sector, record your answers to the following questions:

- Are the walkways (or patio, deck, steps, front stoop, retaining walls, parking area) in good condition?
- Are the walkways wide enough? Are they the right size for my family's lifestyle? Do we need more space?

- Is the shape of the walkways (patio, deck) boring?
- Are the materials they are made from satisfactory and easy to care for? Are they boring (e.g., concrete)?
- Is the parking area large enough?
- Is the fencing in good shape and placed the way I want or need it to be? Do I need more fencing for kids, pets, pool, privacy?

The big picture of your yard is as important as the details. Take a step back and look at the yard space, paying attention to how all of the components work together. Here are a few issues to consider.

- Do I have enough trees or too many?
- Are the trees healthy? Do they need pruning to get them looking presentable?
- Is there enough privacy between my yard and the neighbors' yard?
- Is the whole lawn healthy and green? Does it have sparse areas or wet areas? Does it take a lot of my time to keep it looking good?

- Is there enough lawn for the play and recreation activities of my family? Is there too much lawn for me to handle?

Now it is time to evaluate how your yard fits into the neighborhood and with the style of your house. Then you will be able to put all the pieces together and begin rebuilding your landscape.

Your Neighborhood, Your House

Thirty years ago, little attention was paid to the look of the neighborhood as a whole. Various styles and sizes of houses were built next to each other. Zoning laws were not as strict about lot sizes, setbacks, and outbuildings as they are today. Drainage and grading of properties and streets were not consistent from lot to lot. Wetlands were filled to make building lots, and trees and native plants were removed willy-nilly. On the other hand, the neighborhood didn't look like a cookie-cutter assembly—like so many do today. For these reasons you must look at your neighborhood as a whole and consider your family's lifestyle to determine how to approach your landscaping.

To evaluate the neighborhood, ask yourself the following questions and record them in your diary:
- What style is my house?
- What style are my neighbors' houses?
- Do my neighbors have family situations similar to mine?
- How does the size and layout of my yard and house compare with my neighbors'?
- Is the neighborhood urban, suburban, country? Is it historic?
- Does the neighborhood look and feel formal or informal?
- Does one yard blend into the next or are there divisions or grading differences between the properties?

- Are there wooded areas surrounding the properties or is all the space manicured?
- Is privacy an issue?

Evaluate the degree of formality in your neighborhood. Formality is as much about feel as it is about looks. For example, a neighborhood full of young families has a different feel from a neighborhood full of retirees. Usually the atmosphere in a family-filled neighborhood is more relaxed and informal. There is more interaction among neighbors. The yards are sometimes used commonly among families as the children play together. Plantings are not as precious either in their design or in their need for upkeep. The yards are planned for Saturday's touch football game and barbecue. But once the children leave home, the neighborhood may change and become more formal in lifestyle and plantings.

More often than not, however, neighborhoods are in constant transition; they may lean one way for a number of years and the other way for a while or be all mixed up in their attitudes about landscaping. You will probably feel compelled to do what blends in with the neighborhood, and this may end up being a happy mix of formal and informal in some sectors of your yard.

The informal walkway and plantings match the relaxed style of this cottage home. These neighborhood homes are separated by trees, which allow each house to have its own unique landscape. (Photo by Lee Anne White; © The Taunton Press, Inc.)

Older neighborhoods often have individual styles of architecture and landscaping. Look at your neighborhood as a whole to determine what approach to take in your yard.
(Photo by Boyd Hagan; © The Taunton Press, Inc.)

and informal, more casual landscaping can take over the backyard and real living spaces of the yard.

If you're trying to find good landscaping ideas to fit your house style or if you have a historic house, it's worth your time to do some research. You'll discover what type of landscaping design and materials were commonly used with houses such as yours when that style was first introduced, which can save you a lot of time that you might spend creating a planting plan and choosing each plant. The only caveat is that many plants used long ago have since been improved for their resistance to diseases and insects, hardiness, compact size, and flower color. It also may be difficult to find certain antique cultivars and species because they are no longer grown or not grown in quantity. The new, improved plants still give you the look you want because they are in the same family of plants, with the added benefit of reduced maintenance and greater longevity.

Two popular house styles are Colonial and Victorian (see pp. 12-15 for landscape plans for each). They are reproducible throughout the country, whether your home is authentic to the era or not. These landscape styles also will work for other types of architecture, whether your home is ranch, Tudor, or contemporary.

WHAT'S YOUR STYLE?

House style has influence on formality as well, but only if you want to adhere strictly to what its architectural style demands. There is no rule that says a Georgian-style house must have formal landscaping, especially if it doesn't fit with your lifestyle, although the Georgian style of architecture lends itself well to a formal design.

A formal design has equally balanced plantings on either side of the front door with many close-cropped hedges and evergreens. Often formal gardens are laid out in grids and require a great deal of maintenance to keep them in check. Your taste may run more toward the cottage garden fend-for-itself school of landscaping that is at home with ranch, Colonial, and contemporary styles of architecture. But it doesn't mean you can't have both. Formal gardens can be relegated to the front of the house

Budgeting Time and Money for Renovation

Since there is rarely an unlimited landscaping budget, it is important to decide what your goals are for the project and to prioritize them. If you've just moved into a house and plan to be there as your children grow, you'll probably want to take the time and money to tackle several major projects to make the yard truly yours. If this is a second home or

Even a wooded and shady yard benefits from a neat, manicured appearance. (Photo courtesy *Fine Gardening* magazine; © The Taunton Press, Inc.)

you're getting ready to sell your house, you probably just want to improve the yard's general appearance. In any case, be realistic about how much time and money you can devote to landscaping improvements and how extensive you want them to be.

QUICK AND (RELATIVELY) CHEAP FIXES

If you are only interested in a return on your investment and are selling your property soon, you may just want to tidy up the yard. The basic cleanup, which can be done over a few weekends, includes raking leaves, cutting new edges on the planting beds, and putting new mulch in the beds. This is going to cost you some sweat equity and a little mulch.

Take the cleanup one step further and you will be pruning and moving or removing what is overgrown, which may require a

season's worth of work because certain plants may need to be moved or pruned at certain times of the year. Pruning is done with basic tools that may be expensive, but unless you need the help of a pro, it is still a relatively cheap fix. Rejuvenating the lawn is another route to go and may also require a season to complete. You'll need fertilizer, seed, lime, tools, and possibly topsoil, which can be costly.

Another relatively quick fix is facelifting the landscaping on one side of your house (usually the front), which can be done all at once or, at most, over a growing season. Reusing your existing plants can save money. If you need to augment them with new ones, it can be pricey. Regardless of which quick fix you choose, there is no question that a renovated landscape, even a rudimentary one, will improve the value of your home by as much as 20 percent and make your house sell faster if you are in the market.

This formal foundation planting has clipped hedges and all-white flowers, even on the vine over the door. (Photo by Maureen Gilmer.)

The Colonial Landscape

Early Colonial gardens were more about practicality than ornament. Early settlers planted herbs, vegetables, and fruits, which they brought over by ship from home and gathered from the forests and fields of the New World. They learned remedies from the native Americans and planted medicinal herbs and plants useful for keeping house. The gardens typically were accessible to the kitchen and were planted without design or style.

In later years, well-to-do colonialists in America landscaped their estates to parallel their English counterparts. Less wealthy homeowners created orderly kitchen gardens and floriferous dooryards, influenced by their heritage. Colonial gardens were laid out in grids to make access simple and maintenance easy.

Often surrounded by well-clipped low hedges and geometrically divided with walkways, the gardens were filled with plants chosen from the hundreds of species sent from Europe as well as the native species found in America.

Gardens were planted in patches, usually in the dooryard or front of the house, with vegetables, flowers, herbs, and fruits planted together. Flower and herb drying and making potpourri were favorite pastimes of colonial women. Large crops and orchards were usually a distance from the house, so as not to take up valuable workspace in the back yard.

Lawn areas were small before mechanical cutting equipment was invented, and all cutting was done with hand scythes. The

Colonial Garden Plan

A Colonial garden incorporated vegetables, fruits, and herbs.

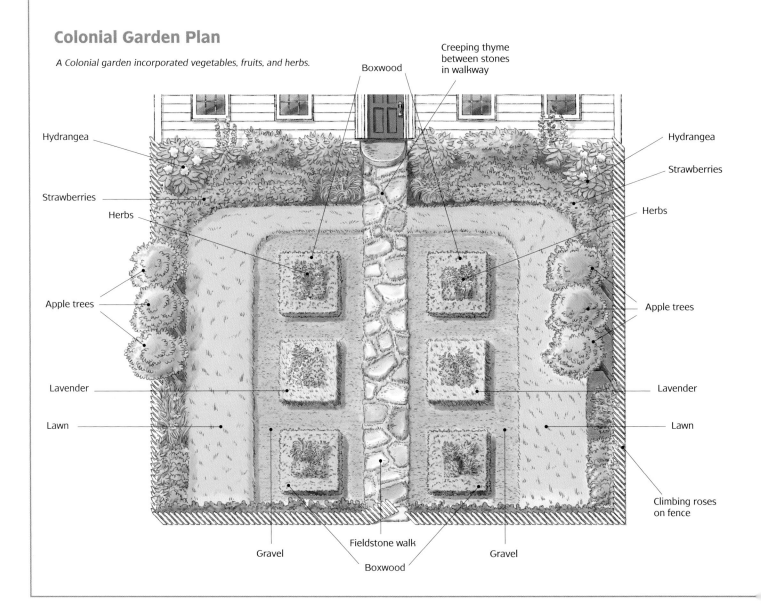

Boxwood

Creeping thyme between stones in walkway

Hydrangea

Strawberries

Herbs

Apple trees

Lavender

Lawn

Hydrangea

Strawberries

Herbs

Apple trees

Lavender

Lawn

Climbing roses on fence

Gravel

Fieldstone walk

Gravel

Boxwood

Early Colonial landscapes were symmetrical and orderly, with grid systems of gardens laid out in the yard and perennials lining the walkways. (Photo by Boyd Hagan; © The Taunton Press, Inc.)

picket fence was used for ornament, but also to corral animals. Often, fences were lush with climbing roses or honeysuckle or used as backdrops for perennials and annuals.

A "contemporary" Colonial garden is laid out in orderly fashion with masses of flowers in grids and low clipped hedges surrounding them. Brick walks make access easy from all sides. Often herb gardens are planted instead of flowers, and a mix of flowers and herbs is not uncommon. Attention is paid to herbs and flowers that are good for drying. Larger shrubs and trees are planted away from the foundation, and picket fences are used as division between yards and as supports for climbing vines.

Colonial Plant List

SHRUBS	HERBS	PERENNIALS AND ANNUALS
Azalea	Basil	Black-eyed Susan
Boxwood	Caraway	Columbine
Honeysuckle	Catnip	Daffodil
Lilac	Chives	Delphinium
Mock orange	Dill	Hollyhock
Rose	Fennel	Lavender
Climbing	Hyssop	Nasturtium
Damask	Mint	Peony
Moss	Sage	Phlox
Scotch	Tarragon	Tulip
Viburnum	Thyme	Turk's cap lily

LONG-TERM PROJECTS

If you plan to remain in your home for a long time, you may want to tackle long-term projects, such as making over the plantings in your yard, improving the hardscaping, or cleaning out an adjacent wooded area. These are jobs that require more of your time and/or more from your wallet.

Although it is time-consuming, making over your whole planting scheme is probably the easiest project to which to assign a time-line and budget—it's a simple task to divide the work and phase it out to make the least impact on your budget and time. Decide what you can spend for phase 1 and pick out the number of plants you can get for your money. You can divide the plantings by sides of the house, by putting in major shrubs first, or by any number of other ways. You can use the techniques in this book to help you make the decisions necessary for accomplishing this task.

Attacking the hardscaping in your yard, such as improving a walkway or patio, is a project with an end, but it can be one of the most costly jobs because of site preparation and materials. Increasing the size or changing the shape of these elements are bigger jobs than filling cracks or facing an existing patio with another material, but any of them takes planning and preparation. You usually cannot stretch this type of project over a long period because prepared areas may be damaged by weather, people, or animals.

Rejuvenating your wooded areas is time-consuming. It requires the proper timing for pruning, which may involve several seasons. You may need a professional arborist to cut down trees, which can be costly, and once the jobs of tree cutting, pruning, and brush cutting are done, you will need to rent machinery to chip brush and split wood or pay for trucking to haul it all away. This is an ongoing project because trees and brush continue to grow.

The Victorian Landscape

The so-called Victorian house was built during the Victorian era from 1850 to 1890. The style has been copied for decades, so it is possible to buy a Victorian-style house that was built in the 1900s. Classically, a Victorian has a fancy facade with ornate woodworking, but many Victorians are simple two-story affairs with a porch on the front and clapboard siding.

The typical Victorian was spare in its use of foundation plants. This was based on the fear of illness brought on by the excessive humidity and shade the plants would impart by creating dark and damp places around the home. In addition, and more substantiated, it was thought that insects and decay would debilitate the house because of the humidity. The builders were proud of their handiwork and beautiful, artfully built stone foundations, which weren't in need of hiding. Vines were used on the porches, and often tall evergreen shrubs were used on either side of the walk as it approached the house or to flank the front door.

Flowers were beloved by the Victorians, and perennials and annuals were used on the sides of the house in small gardens. The theory of landscaping was that it should be viewed from inside the house looking out; the house was the focal point and the plantings were subordinate in their scheme.

Victorian Garden Plan

Victorian gardens were symmetrical.

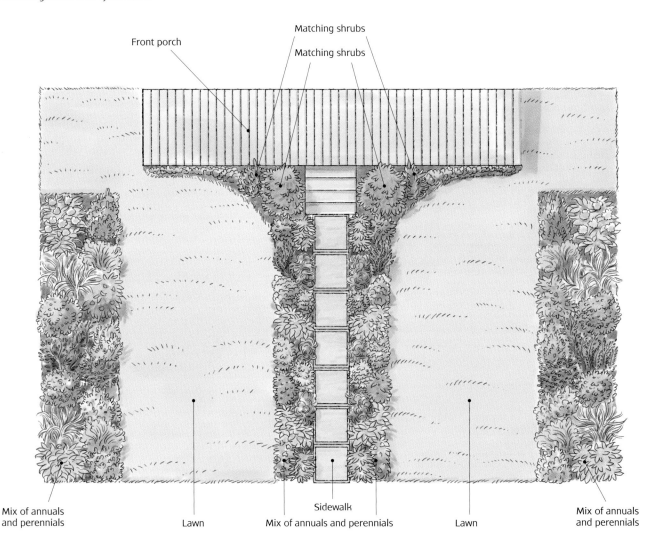

Front porch

Matching shrubs

Matching shrubs

Mix of annuals and perennials

Lawn

Sidewalk

Mix of annuals and perennials

Lawn

Mix of annuals and perennials

Victorian plantings were spare because it was believed that plants near houses would deteriorate the house and not allow for air movement, causing human illness. A few perennials along the foundation or porch was enough adornment. (Photo by Boyd Hagan; © The Taunton Press, Inc.)

Victorian Plant List

SHRUBS	VINES	PERENNIALS AND ANNUALS
Andromeda	Clematis	Ageratum
Azalea	Dutchman's-pipe	Alyssum
Barberry	Honeysuckle	Aster
Boxwood	Ivy	Coreopsis
Daphne	Morning glory	Daylily
Forsythia	Trumpet vine	Delphinium
Holly	Virginia creeper	Dusty miller
Hydrangea	Wisteria	Hardy
Lilac		chrysanthemum
Mock orange		Hosta
Peony		Shasta daisy
Privet		Veronica
Quince		Yarrow
Rhododendron		
Rose		
Spiraea		
Viburnum		

ADDING IT ALL UP

Once you have determined the scale of the project, you can price it out. First, decide what you can do yourself and what you'll leave to the pros. Then cost out the materials for your own projects and get estimates from contractors. With budget in hand, it should be evident from your evaluation of the neighborhood if you are improving beyond its standards or beyond the value of what your house demands.

If it is not evident to you, consult with a real estate professional. He can do a comparison of other homes in the neighborhood. This information will help you decide what you want or need and help you make intelligent decisions about any overimprovements. For instance, if you want a pool, you can find out from a realtor not only that there are others in the neighborhood but also that you'd be better off putting in a reasonably priced vinyl-lined pool than a custom gunnite pool.

Let's Get Started!

In the ensuing chapters, you will learn about all of these projects and more. First, I will tackle the live elements: plants around your house foundation, the perimeters of your yard, and wooded areas. You will learn how to identify what plants you have and how to make decisions about what plants to keep, move, and discard. You will find out about basic design techniques and how to use your existing landscaping to reshape the character of your yard. Advice on renovating hardscaping elements will help you make your backyard into an outdoor room.

Finally, you will choose from finishing touches that put your hallmark on the job and turn an ordinary house with landscaping into a home with a livable, inviting yard and gardens.

2 Keepers, Movers, and Composters

Whether you have specific plans for your yard or you simply know it needs a facelift, the starting point is the same: Assess your plants. Like looking in the fridge to see what's available before you start cooking, it's important to see what's already growing in your yard before you create a plan. Unlike new construction, where you begin with a clean slate, renovation starts with trying to work with what exists. Consequently, you must decide what elements and plants are worth the effort of keeping, even if they need sprucing up. This requires some simple decisions and a bit of research.

Your ultimate goal is a well-designed landscape, which includes the elements shown here: plantings in scale with the house, texture and color changes, vertical as well as horizontal interest, and serpentine beds. (Photo by Scott Gibson; © The Taunton Press, Inc.)

The first step involves taking a good look at your plants. Using only your initial impressions and feelings, sort your existing plants into three categories: keepers, movers, and composters.

Keepers are plants that are beautiful and thriving in their present location. They have few or no pests or diseases, you like where they're located, and, with a bit of pruning, they can look even better.

Movers are healthy plants that need to find another place in the yard. Often they are overgrown, need different growing conditions like more sunlight, or would enhance the yard in another location. Or perhaps you can't bear the thought of cutting down your favorite tree, but your family wants to install a patio where the tree now stands. You can probably move the tree to another location.

Composters are common plants that are dying, unappealing to you, or cannot be salvaged through pruning. They may be older hybrids or cultivars that are susceptible to insects and diseases, and you suspect there are better plants to take their places in the landscape.

To select your keepers, movers, and composters, take a walk around your yard and ask yourself these questions. Make notes in your diary.
- Do I like this plant?
- Is this plant healthy? Does it have insects or diseases?
- Has this plant been pruned regularly and properly?
- Is this plant too close to the house?
- Does this plant have the right habit for its location? (Habit refers to whether it hugs the ground, spreads wide, grows upright, or weeps toward the ground.)
- Does this plant flower well? (If not, it may be a sun-loving plant in too shady a spot.)
- Does this plant block any windows?
- Would I rather have another feature (flower bed, walkway, patio, etc.) where this plant is growing?

Name That Plant

Now it's time for a bit of research. Before you decide whether to make a plant the centerpiece of your front yard or toss it on the compost heap, you need more information about it. Find out each of your plants' names, their growing requirements, and any unique features about them. If you know what a plant is, you can read about its characteristics and make informed decisions about it. If you do not know what your plants are, you will have to learn how to identify them or call in your local extension agent or other expert for help.

Identifying plants can be done at any time of year, but it requires more expertise to "read" buds and twigs than to identify a plant in full leaf and flower. Therefore, if you begin the identification process when a deciduous plant has lost its leaves, it may be necessary to wait until it comes to life in the spring to verify your results. You can record your observations about a plant in the winter, but, generally speaking, plant identification is more easily done when the plant is actively growing.

In order to accurately identify your plants, you'll need to note their characteristics. These are listed in order of the most elemental characteristics to the most detailed.

1. Is the plant deciduous (loses its leaves each fall) or evergreen (always has leaves or needles)? Are the stems of the plant woody or herbaceous (green and soft)?
2. Determine the habit (growth shape) of the plant. Is it upright, weeping, ground-hugging, or wide-spreading?
3. Using a good plant encyclopedia, identify the bud and stem characteristics.
4. Examine the bark's color and texture. Is it peeling, smooth, or furrowed?
5. Look at the leaves and compare them to those shown in your plant encyclopedia.
6. Note the flower characteristics: color, shape, arrangement, time of bloom.

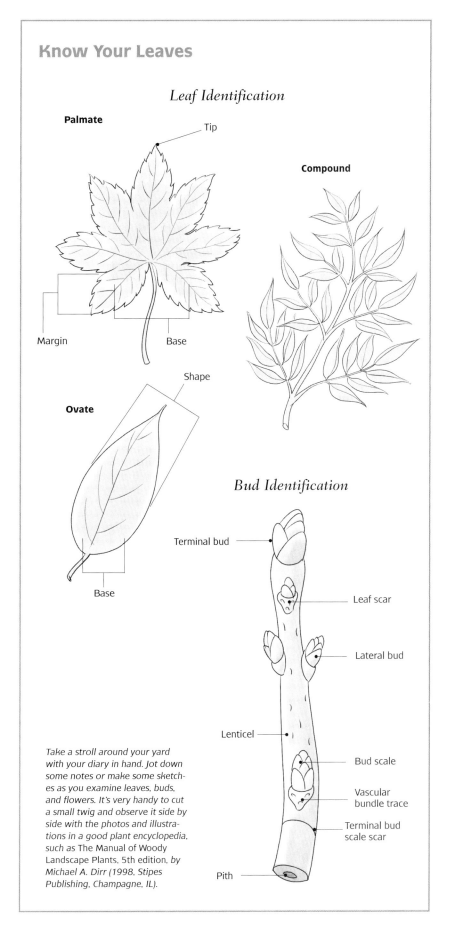

Know Your Leaves

Leaf Identification

Palmate
Tip
Margin
Base

Compound

Ovate
Shape
Base

Bud Identification

Terminal bud
Leaf scar
Lateral bud
Lenticel
Bud scale
Vascular bundle trace
Terminal bud scale scar
Pith

Take a stroll around your yard with your diary in hand. Jot down some notes or make some sketches as you examine leaves, buds, and flowers. It's very handy to cut a small twig and observe it side by side with the photos and illustrations in a good plant encyclopedia, such as The Manual of Woody Landscape Plants, 5th edition, by Michael A. Dirr (1998, Stipes Publishing, Champaign, IL).

7. See if the plant bears fruit. If it does, note its characteristics: color, shape, size, arrangement, time of year it bears fruit.

Plant color is an obvious distinguishing factor, but be aware that color of leaves and flowers, size of leaves, and size of the plant as a whole may all fluctuate depending on growing conditions. If certain elements are lacking in the soil, the flower or leaf color may be off or may be completely different from the encyclopedia description. For example, certain hydrangeas growing in acid soil produce blue flowers but in basic soils, the flowers are pink. Lack of nitrogen will cause leaves to be lighter green than described in an encyclopedia.

If a plant is thirsting for water, the leaves may be smaller than usual. If you live in a very cold climate, the plant may not reach its potential size as described in a plant encyclopedia. So don't take the words of the plant encyclopedia verbatim. The only sure way to identify plants is with study and experience or the advice of an expert.

Using the plant's distinguishing characteristics, find its botanical name in a good plant encyclopedia. Read about its normal habit, ultimate size and spread, flower color (if applicable), hardiness zone, rate of growth, soil requirements, maintenance needs, disease and insect susceptibility, and whether it likes sun, shade, or partial shade. List these characteristics for each plant in your diary. You can organize the list in many ways. For instance, you can put all shade-loving plants together, all tall (over 6 ft.) plants together, all evergreens together, or however makes the best sense to you.

The color of hydrangea flowers is reactive to the pH of the soil in which the plant grows. The blue hydrangea in the foreground has been fertilized with aluminum sulphate, which adjusts the soil pH lower or more acid, causing the flowers to turn blue. The pink hydrangea in the background indicates that the native soil has a basic pH, and must be adjusted to have blue flowers.
(Photo © Alan and Linda Detrick.)

What's in a Name?

The modern-day system of plant names is credited to Carl von Linné, aka Linnaeus. It is known as the Linnaean system of binomial nomenclature. Each plant is given a two-part Latin name. It is by this name that people all over the world know a plant, regardless of country or language spoken. Classification of plants is important for consistency around the globe because common names for plants vary from one country to another and even within countries. The first part of a plant name is known as the *genus* of the plant, and the second is the *specific epithet*. Together they are the *species* or *species name*. For instance, the species *Syringa vulgaris*, common lilac, has a genus name of *Syringa* and a specific epithet of *vulgaris*.

The genus is basically one or more species of plant that are closely related. There may be many *genera* (plural of genus) within a family of plants. The genus name always begins with a capital letter and is either underlined or italicized. It may be shortened to the first letter and period (*S. vulgaris*) if used following the spelled-out genus name. A genus name may stand alone or be followed by sp. (abbreviation for species) or spp. (more than one species) if a specific epithet is not being named.

The specific epithet is often descriptive of a certain characteristic or concept about the plant. In this case, *vulgaris* means "common." Another lilac species, *Syringa microphylla*, means "little leaf" lilac. The abbreviation var. after a species name indicates a variety of the species, as in *Syringa reticulata* var. *mandschurica*. The name describes this tree lilac as a variety discovered in Manchuria.

You may also see an x between the genus name and specific epithet, which means the plant is a hybrid, or cross of plants. *Syringa x chinensis* is a hybrid between the plants *S. persica* and *S. vulgaris*, although you wouldn't be able to determine the parentage of the hybrid by looking at the name.

Your diary is a good organizational tool to help you determine which plants to keep, and, if you are keeping them, whether they need to be moved and where to move them. You may uncover a few surprises as you do your research, so compare your initial "keeper, mover, composter" list with this new information. For example, you may find that a plant you weren't very attached to is uncommon, which may make you decide to keep it.

What to Keep

A keeper plant is healthy, full of leaves, free of insects and disease, and has inherent insect and disease resistance. It has been maintained over the years, so it is not overgrown or improperly pruned. It is easy to maintain and appropriate for the bed you plan to keep it in. In other words, it will not grow too large and does not need to be severely and frequently pruned in order to maintain its size.

A keeper plant grows the way you want it to: upright, weeping, spreading, or hugging the ground. The flower color works with your scheme, and the plant blooms over a long period of time or at a time of year that alternates or is compatible with other plants in the bed. The plant will easily survive the winter (a characteristic known as hardiness) without needing extraordinary protection each winter to keep it alive. It has no special soil requirements or is compatible with the type of soil you have (i.e., acid, basic, heavy clay, sandy). Shade-loving plants are in a northern or eastern exposure and sun-loving plants are living in west- or south-facing beds. You may decide to keep a plant for sentimental reasons, but be sure it is truly happy in its present location by studying its cultural requirements as documented in a plant encyclopedia.

Many people enjoy the company of birds and other wildlife, and you may decide to keep a plant or a group of plants

where they are situated because they attract wildlife to that area. This is a logical decision, but be careful about keeping a wildlife habitat too close to your house, even though the temptation is great to be able to watch through your windows. Not only are the animals and birds happier when they are left undisturbed, but this will also prevent your house from becoming the animals' domain. Male woodpeckers love to peck holes in siding when they mate, many landscape plants are a staple of deer diets, and bees and wasps love scented, colorful flowers as much as but-

This flowering crape myrtle will stay in scale and never need to be moved because it was properly situated to begin with. (Photo by Maureen Gilmer.)

Create interest in a planting bed by combining color and texture. In this bed, the variety of colored foliage—red, light green, dark green, variegated yellow with green, and white with green—keeps the bed attractive even after flowers have faded. The texture change also keeps the bed interesting. (Photo by Boyd Hagan; © The Taunton Press, Inc.)

terflies and hummingbirds do. So unless the habitat poses no threat to *your* habitat, plants for wildlife should be moved to an area away from human activity.

What to Move

Upon examining the plants in your diary, you may see that there are plants you want to keep, but they are in the wrong place. They may need more or less sun, more room to grow without severe pruning, or more plants around them to grow their best. Don't give up on these plants. The design of your planting plan can be created around them, perhaps with a few new additions, because you are not restricted to the positions they hold in the landscape now. Most plants can be moved easily to other parts of the yard where they will be happier in a new exposure or with more breathing room, or they can be moved within a planting bed to freshen the scheme.

There are several reasons for moving plants to new locations. First, you may have been pruning a particular plant for years to keep it to a certain size. If it is a constant battle, that plant may be better off in another part of the yard where it can grow to its potential. Or you may have wondered why a plant does not flower well or flower at all. It may need a different exposure, sun or shade, or may have been shaded out by taller plants you are now removing. It will perform best if moved to a different bed or a different position within the bed.

Relocating plants may also make your yard more beautiful year-round. For example, if the bed has been filled with all evergreens or all the same deciduous plant, you will want to move some of them to other beds and mix in new colors, shapes, and textures.

Plants with Four-Season Appeal

Left: Choose landscape plants with a variety of bloom times so they offer year-round or four-season appeal. The bark of sycamore trees puts on a show year-round. (Photo by Chris Curless; © The Taunton Press, Inc.)

Right: Witchhazel blooms early in the season, offering a jolt of color to the winter landscape. (Photo by Susan Roth; © The Taunton Press, Inc.)

Below: Harry Lauder's walking stick is a living sculpture in winter. In spring it has catkin-like flowers, and for the rest of the year it twists and turns with branches of large green leaves. (Photo by Steve Silk; © The Taunton Press, Inc.)

Two Types of Foundation Planting Beds

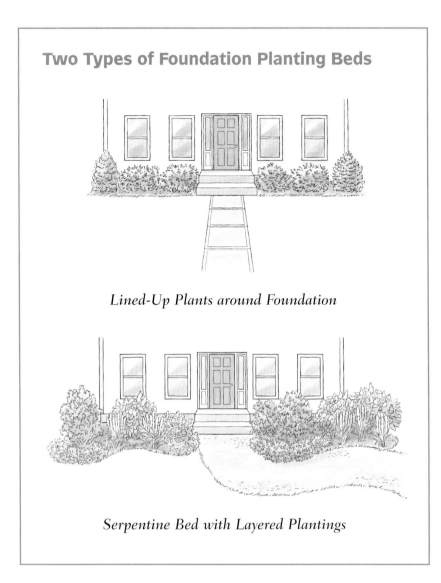

Lined-Up Plants around Foundation

Serpentine Bed with Layered Plantings

Improper pruning and removal of a neighboring plant caused this spreading yew to lose most of its bottom leaves. Sun cannot reach lower branches when plants are pruned with the top wider than the bottom. This plant is a candidate for the compost heap. (Photo by Boyd Hagan; © The Taunton Press, Inc.)

Further, a good plan includes plants with four-season appeal. This is particularly important in the front-yard garden or near walkways and patios where they will be seen. If a plant is only attractive in spring flower, it should be placed where it can be appreciated for that season and will not take up valuable show space in other seasons when it is not so interesting. In its place, a plant with fall leaf color, fall and winter berries, and/or winter sculptural twigs as well as spring or summer flowers would be a better choice.

Even if your plants are in the right planting bed, you might want to consider giving them a new arrangement. Plantings in rigid lines surrounding the foundation can be redesigned to create a serpentine bed that softens the harsh lines of the walls of the house. This will create more planting space and allow for a layered scheme with taller plants toward the back; middle-sized shrubs to the center; and low shrubs, perennials, and ground covers in front, following the shape of the bed.

Moving plants you want to keep must be done carefully, at the right stage in their growth cycle, and in a timely fashion (see Chapter 8, beginning on p. 94). You should be prepared for losses when you are transplanting. Twenty percent loss is not unreasonable, but you can cut your losses by transplanting only healthy, vital plants. It may require more than one growing season to move all the plants you want to, especially if weather conditions slow or speed up the seasons. The ground may not be conducive to digging when you need it to be to safely transplant a certain species. For instance, most deciduous trees and shrubs should be transplanted before they leaf out in spring or after they drop their leaves in fall. Should the ground be frozen or too wet, you may miss your window.

This twig has been damaged by a borer-type insect. The area must be pruned off just below the damage at the next bud where the wood is intact. (Photo courtesy the University of Connecticut.)

What to Compost

Determining what should be composted is in many ways a subjective process, but some common reasons for composting can help guide your decision. First, the plant is a candidate for the compost heap when it is dead or near dead.

Second, if it was planted close to another plant and has become one-sided (either unshapely or even dead where it touched the other plant), pruning may be insufficient to reshape the plant, short of cutting it to the ground and waiting for seasons or years for it to rejuvenate.

Third, insect or disease damage may kill parts of a plant, causing it to be one-sided or misshapen. Swollen sections of a branch indicate a borer has been wreaking havoc, whereas sunken, soft cankers signal the presence of insects with sucking mouthparts.

Any lumps, bumps, or dark spots should be pruned out (see Chapter 7, beginning on p. 78), and the affected parts

should be bagged and discarded. Pruning may not be enough to save a plant infested with critters. An infested plant is under a lot of stress and will never perform the way it should. If a plant is very susceptible to insects or disease, that alone may be reason to chuck it. The good news is that in recent years many pest-susceptible plants have been hybridized to breed resistance into their genes, and you can enjoy the same plants (usually with different cultivar names) pest-free.

Improper pruning is another reason to discard a plant. Some plants, especially evergreens such as yews, are often pruned improperly, resulting in poor shape and lack of exposure to sunlight. The green meatball shape that tapers in toward the middle and bottom of the plant blocks sunlight from reaching those parts, which causes it to lose leaves and die out where the sun doesn't shine on it. Personally, I would send it to the compost heap because it probably will take many years, if ever, to recover if left alone and, in the meantime, it looks half-dead.

Deciduous plant pruning mistakes will be most obvious when the leaves have dropped. Along roadsides under electric wires you'll often see trees that have been butchered by inexperienced linemen. A

This stem has a canker and must be pruned off. Pinch or prune below the damage at the next bud. (Photo courtesy the University of Connecticut.)

High-Maintenance Plants

Some plants can be consigned to the compost heap because they're just plain messy and a pain to clean up after. Weak-wooded plants like willows constantly drop pieces of themselves with only the slightest breeze. Some plants drop fruit, which is messy and attracts bees and insects to the yard. Others are invasive and reroot throughout the garden. Below is a list of some of the most common high-maintenance plants. Unless you are in love with them, I would suggest that you remove them from your yard.

American bittersweet (*Celastrus scandens*)	Kills and girdles everything in its way.
Black walnut (*Juglans nigra*)	Emits a substance called juglone from all plant parts into the soil; many other plants will not survive near or under where it is planted.
Dwarf bamboo (*Arundinaria pygmaea*)	Invasive; use caution in siting all hardy bamboos.
Hawthorn (*Crataegus spp.*)	Long, 2-in. thorns are dangerous; severely affected by insects and diseases.
Hickory (*Carya* spp.)	Difficult to transplant; messy droppings of leaves, stems, fruit.
Hopa, Almey, and Eleyi crabapples (*Malus* 'Hopa', *M.* 'Almey', *M.* 'Eleyi')	Very susceptible to disease.
Japanese honeysuckle (*Lonicera japonica*)	Very competitive; shades out and twines around everything in its way; many other species of honeysuckle are susceptible to insects.
Trumpet vine (*Campsis radicans*)	Climbs over everything in its way; grows anywhere.
Virginia creeper (*Parthenocissus quinquefolia*)	Twines and spreads like crazy; use only if all else fails.
Weeping willow (*Salix alba* 'Tristis' and others)	Dirty street tree; invasive roots.

tree exposed to constant, reckless, mis timed pruning will show considerable damage in the shape of the head because it reacts to the pruning with lots of vigorous growth. When this is repeatedly hacked off, it leaves an unsightly mess of knobby, stubby branches. Stubby branches, sometimes with witch's broom-like shapes at their tips, are a sure sign of either improper pruning techniques or insect damage.

You may have plants in your yard that you just don't like. If they are in good shape, you can ask your neighbors and friends if they are interested in these unwanted plants. But to avoid making enemies, offer them lunch, a cool drink, transportation, and tools, and let them dig it up and remove it to their own yard. If it dies, it won't be your fault, and if it lives, you'll both be happy.

Removing plants you don't want is fairly easy (see p. 47) and can be done at any time, but it always has to be done with caution. The easiest way is to cut them to the ground with a saw, pruners, loppers, or chain saw, depending on the size of the plant. Dig out the roots with a pick, ax, or shovel. Unless you are trained to take down large trees and are skilled with a chain saw, I suggest that you leave the job to a licensed arborist or landscaping professional, who can also grind out the stump and chip the brush.

Plants that aren't big enough for chipping, such as small shrubs and herbaceous perennials, may be suitable for composting. Their sacrifice can become a rich contribution to the soil in your garden. Include household scraps (except meat and bones), leaves, and grass clippings in your compost pile. All organic materials will break down eventually, but avoid large branches and stumps because they will take forever. Chip them first and add the chips and sawdust to the heap. Putting unwanted plants in the compost pile is better than adding them directly to the garden because, as they broke down in the garden, they would rob precious nitrogen from the soil.

If you compost diseased or insect-infested plants, be sure to allow the compost heap to mature fully before using it. The high temperatures that eventually build up in the compost pile will kill the

A compost bin is easily fashioned out of wood and wire and is most convenient if situated near the garden. (Photo © Alan and Linda Detrick.)

culprits, but if you steal from the pile before it is ready, you may spread those dreaded diseases before they meet their demise. The moist, warm composting environment can be just the fuel some diseases need to proliferate.

Starting Your Compost Pile

Before you begin composting, you'll need a bin to contain your compost pile. There are bins available at garden centers made from various materials and in several sizes, or you can make your own from wooden slats or chicken wire.

Start your pile with 6 in. of yard and kitchen waste. Then add a 2-in. layer of soil on top. Continue alternating layers of waste and soil. You can add lime to the layers to speed up decomposition. Turn the pile once a month with a pitchfork or shovel. This helps everything break down faster. The pile also needs moisture, so make sure the top of the pile is concave to catch rainwater.

During decomposition, the center of the pile will heat up to as much as 150°F. This temperature is high enough to kill microorganisms and diseases that may be in your yard waste. The compost is ready to use when all the elements are completely decomposed.

3 Developing the Yard: Dreaming and Planning

You've assessed how your yard fits into your neighborhood. You've evaluated the specific needs you have for your outdoor spaces and looked at your house and yard for style compatibility. The next step in the makeover of your yard is to define the different spaces that make up the whole yard. These spaces may be as large as a play area or orchard or as small and detailed as the foundation planting. The key is to work from the largest divisions down to the smaller, more detailed areas, identifying the projects you want to take on and drafting a plan to complete them.

A large, open, well-manicured yard with perimeter plantings separates this yard from the neighbor's. (Photo © Alan and Linda Detrick.)

Many suburban home- owners protect their privacy by leaving wild space between them and their neigh- bors. (Photo by Boyd Hagan; © The Taunton Press, Inc.)

There are several issues to consider during this process, including how large the mani- cured portion of the yard should be, where to replant the shrubs and perennials you have decided to keep, what new plants to add, and what permanent features to aug- ment or add. In this chapter, I will discuss how to determine what is manicured and what is wild space in the yard, what will be family living spaces for both the long and short term, prioritizing and scheduling the various projects in the yard, and mapping out your dream yard.

Well-Tended or Wild?

There are no hard and fast rules about how much of the yard should be cultivated with plantings and lawn and how much can be left to its own devices. Some of the decision is dictated by the location of your house. In the city or suburban neighborhood, you may feel pressured to maintain the perfect yard. If lawn meets lawn from lot to lot, leaving some areas in a more natural state may spoil the pristine look of the neighborhood.

In rural areas, the choice of how much yard to cultivate and how much to leave "wild" may be an easy one if there is clear definition between the two areas; for exam- ple, mowed and unmowed spaces or spaces framed by planting beds. The decision of

how much lawn to mow is a personal one dependent on whether you like to mow, whether a lawn service does the work for you, or if your yard is the neighborhood ball field. As your family grows up or you grow tired of mowing, you can downsize the lawn space.

Current wisdom recommends leaving "wild" space in your yard for migrating birds, diminishing animal and plant populations, and for capturing water—particularly if this wild space already exists. This will reduce the maintenance needs in your yard as well as the use of chemical fertilizers and excess water because less space is manicured. But low maintenance doesn't mean no mainte- nance. You should care for wild areas with good management techniques because they are important for maintaining a healthy plant and animal population. It's also impor- tant for the uncultivated spaces to be an asset to the neighborhood, not an eyesore.

Many older homes were built in low- lying, swampy areas, which were filled to make building lots before environmental laws were enacted to protect wetlands from development. In the old days, you could turn these unusable parts of the yard into ponds and alter wetlands as you pleased. Today, you must seek permission to alter a wetland, and, in many areas, it is not permitted.

If you have a wet area in your yard, you may be allowed to "clean it up" by removing dead and dying plant life and adding wet- land plants, which will improve the unculti- vated area. But if you alter a wetland with- out permission, you may be fined and required to restore the wetland to its origi- nal location as well as to replant it with the exact plants it supported before it was touched. Contact your state agricultural or environmental agencies to determine wet- land laws and regulations in your state *before* you alter an area.

Family Spaces

Good landscape planning takes careful thought and creativity because you'll need to assess your family's needs now and predict what they'll be in several years. Consider your current lifestyle and prioritize the uses of the areas of the yard, but also think about the future uses of the spaces and plan for them, especially if they affect relatively permanent structures or plantings you may be considering for immediate installation.

For instance, if you intend to install a pool in a few years, it makes no sense to plant a grove of shade trees in the only site where the pool will fit, even though planting the grove will help you reduce the time you spend mowing. Or, if you want to build a children's play yard now, complete with swing set, it can be easily dismantled when the kids are grown. At that time, the yard can be downsized and replaced by a wildflower garden or less developed area.

A wet area in the yard, enhanced with plantings, is transformed from a maintenance nightmare to a featured asset. (Photo by Delilah Smittle; © The Taunton Press, Inc.)

A rustic fence separates the wild, unkempt area of the yard from the maintained space. (Photo by Boyd Hagan; © The Taunton Press, Inc.)

SPECIALIZED AREAS

When space is at a premium, it is still possible to set aside specialized areas in your yard such as manicured and wild sections or to separate recreation areas for children and adults. A small yard must be multipurpose, so the design may have to be altered to allow for many uses. For example, if the existing patio is too small for barbecuing and relaxing with a book at the same time, then the renovation priority may be to enlarge the patio and reduce the lawn space. If your yard is the site of the Saturday morning ball games, adding to the planting area along the periphery and decreasing the size of the lawn is probably not a good idea—instead, maximizing the open space may be the priority.

When there is a need to combine interests in a small space, you do not always have to compromise one for another. For instance, a gardener can have patio and relaxation space and also plant container gardens, window boxes, and trellises for

A play area tucked into the trees is shaded and blends well into the landscape. This yard is not as large as it seems, but the spaces are maximized to accommodate both children and adults. (Photo courtesy *Fine Gardening* magazine; © The Taunton Press, Inc.)

Combine interesting plantings in a small space by using planter boxes and containers. There's still room to relax, and the space is greatly enhanced by the planters. (Photo by Ken Druse.)

climbing plants within the confines of the patio, or play space can be maximized by adding a raised bed for a sandbox right alongside those for your vegetables.

USE YOUR IMAGINATION

No matter what size your yard, let your imagination run wild as you decide on the improvements for a new landscape. Don't feel locked in to the shape, size, or materials now in your yard. Try to visualize your ideal yard, mentally mapping out special-function spaces, changes to hardscape features, and where you'd like to have trees and shrubs, gardens and borders. Take into consideration the plants you've marked to keep, but want to move to another location. As you're doing this, jot down your ideas in your diary for later reference. These notes will be the foundation of a priority list and action plan you'll use to create your dream yard.

From Dreamscape to Landscape: The Plan

After you've spent some time imagining your perfect yard, you'll need to develop a strategy to turn what you've imagined into reality. Developing a working plan is the best way to begin. Making these plans is as fundamental to the project as blueprints are to building a home or a recipe is to cooking dinner.

Your plan should have two components: (1) a prioritized written list of changes and improvements, including action steps necessary; and (2) a sketch of the landscape you want to achieve. You'll probably want to develop the list and the sketch side by side, but let's start with the priority list.

MAKE A PRIORITY LIST

Take the notes you wrote in your diary and arrange them in order of priority. Decide which changes are most crucial for reasons of safety, aesthetics, or personal enjoyment and rank the changes or improvements in order of importance.

Your priority list should also include questions you need to ask yourself before you run out to purchase materials or pull up turf. This may involve a bit of research. You must find out what your projects will involve in terms of time, money, and logistics. Ask yourself the questions listed in "Making a Priority List." If you don't know the answers, find out. Consult your local library or bookstores for reputable do-it-yourself books, call a professional, and check out the local rental center for equipment. Knowing ahead of time what elements your project

Making a Priority List

If you plan to renovate your front yard and/or backyard, this might be an example of your priority list.

1. Enlarge the patio.

2. Thin or replace foundation plantings.

3. Thin and improve landscaping around the pool.

4. Clear section of front woodlot to allow more sun for gardens.

5. Install a vegetable garden in the backyard.

6. Build a fence around the vegetable garden to keep out deer.

7. Rebuild the front door stoop.

8. Install a walkway to the front door.

Questions to Answer

• What steps do I need to take before I can start this project?

• How much time will each project on the list take, and how much time do I have available to devote?

• What can I afford to do now or in the future?

• Can I do the project myself or do I need to hire a pro?

Vegetable Garden Action Plan

Item 5 in "Making a Priority List" (see p. 33) is "install a vegetable garden in the backyard." Here's how you can break down that item into an action plan.

To do	When
• Make a plan of the garden	autumn
• Measure and mark off the area for the garden	autumn
• Strip sod and dig up the beds	autumn
• Have the soil tested	autumn
• Add amendments	autumn
• Decide what to plant	winter
• Order seeds	winter/early spring
• Start seedlings indoors	winter to midspring
• Add amendments	midspring
• Plant outdoor seeds and seedlings	after last frost

Drawing tools are useful for putting ideas on paper. From top to bottom: a pencil sharpener, draftsman's triangle, scales, lead pencil, circle and plant templates, compass, cleaning brush, flexible curve, and masking tape. (Photo by Scott Phillips; © The Taunton Press, Inc.)

will involve, such as grading, tree removal, soil improvement, and the like, will help you create more accurate estimates.

Sometimes a few quick telephone calls or a trip to a home center can help you get your priorities in perspective. Home centers are also sources of ideas and potential solutions. For example, if you want to enlarge your patio, at a home center you'll find patio materials that don't require complicated installation techniques or tools. Given easy-to-use materials, a job that would be too challenging to do yourself suddenly becomes accessible. So investigate options.

Get quotes on materials from several sources and ask for estimates from a professional for complicated jobs like installing a new entranceway. This will help you figure out the trade-offs and evaluate the overall project. You may find that it's more economical to hire a professional, who can buy materials more cheaply and get the job done faster. Meanwhile, you can spend your time doing another project more within your reach.

Break it down

Once you've decided to tackle a project, add action steps to your priority list by breaking the project into smaller tasks. You can make an action plan for each of your priorities and set dates for beginning the projects. You'll quickly be able to see which project needs immediate attention, which can sit on the back burner, and what times of the year you'll be the busiest. An action plan can help keep you from being overwhelmed, especially if you intend to work on several projects at the same time.

MAKE A WORKING MAP OF YOUR YARD

Once you have your projects well planned, make a map of your property as it now exists so you can see what impact the changes will have on your yard. The simplest way is to

A Working Plan with House Measurements

Make a scale drawing of your house before adding landscape features.

take pad and pencil outside and make a line drawing of the yard and house from an overhead view, including the window and door openings.

This does not have to be perfect or done with a T square, but it should be drawn to scale. Use a tape measure to obtain the actual measurements and fill them in on the plan using an architect's or engineer's scale. These rulers reduce the actual measurements incrementally, for instance, 1 in. equals 4 ft. You can also use graph paper, but make sure it has a scale

fine enough to get everything you need to show on the page.

On the paper, draw in your landscape's permanent features, starting with the largest items like the walkway or a hedge. For example, if there is a large, established tree in the foundation planting that you want to keep in place, you will have to build the design around it, so you should sketch in the tree on your map. Only include existing shrubs or perennials or the existing shape of the planting beds if you are sure you will not be changing them.

Now take a piece of tracing paper and lay it over your drawing. On tracing paper, draw in different landscape plans without altering your original map. For each new design, use a new sheet of tracing paper. After you've completed several designs, you can compare their best features.

Start with the walkway and front entry. If you are happy with them as is, draw them in to scale. If changing the walkway is one of your priorities, try drawing it several ways (curved, etc.). Next, place any other permanent features—such as a pool or patio—on your priority list. Try them in different places and in various sizes. Then, move to planting beds and specific plants, keeping in mind which plants you'll keep and how you can reshape the beds. If you are unsure of

Tracing the Features

Once you add landscape features to your scale drawing, place tracing paper over it and draw in landscape variations to try out different designs.

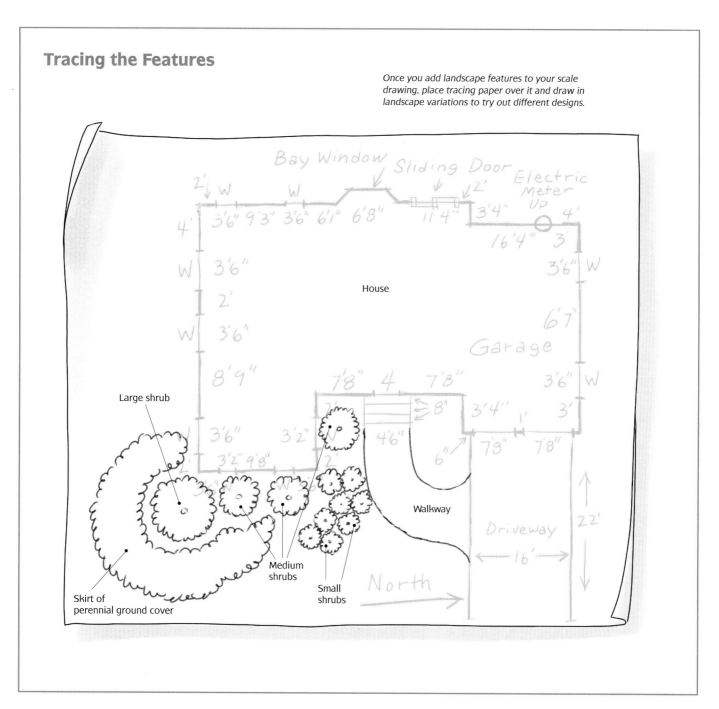

what you have or what you should keep, be as general in your scheme as possible.

Draw circles to scale to represent plants. You can use the architect's or engineer's scale to make the circles the right size or buy a template with circles of the right size. In labeling the circles on the tracing paper, only be as specific as to whether they are evergreen or flowering shrub or perennial. If you want to add a plant that will mature to 6 ft. tall and 4 ft. across, for example, draw a circle with a diameter equivalent to 4 ft. and label it "EVERGREEN 6 ft. x 4 ft." Make bigger circles for the base plants or a specimen tree and circles that run together for ground covers or groups of plants.

Keep drawing until you like the ideas. Move around to all sides of the foundation of the house, and then to the rest of the yard. Map out the spaces you defined earlier like specialty gardens, a dog run, or a play yard. Sketch in a pool or pond if you will be building one. Include screening and fencing and any other elements you are considering. Use a free hand and an open mind and have fun while sketching these ideas into life.

The completed drawing will combine all the best features from the tracing paper drawings with the existing features in the yard as well as any existing features you plan to move from their original spots. You will keep this "blueprint" and refer to it over and over again as you build your landscape.

This curved planting bed complements the walkway, which was designed to flow through it and lead the way to an existing concrete driveway. The garden beds continue on the other side. (Photo by Lee Anne White; © The Taunton Press, Inc.)

4 Reshaping the Wild Spaces

Once you've decided which areas in your yard will be cultivated and which will be left more "natural," you can begin reshaping those areas. Even natural areas need routine upkeep, or they quickly become overgrown. Typically, an open, unmanaged area is taken over by fast-growing softwood saplings that will thin out and give way to hardwood saplings. Although it takes years for the growth to develop into a formidable wooded site, you will be surprised at how quickly the shrubby young saplings spring up.

A woodland garden is carved from the wild to create a fantastic spring show. Later in the season, when the high canopy of tree leaves are full size, this space is a shady respite with meandering paths. (Photo © Alan and Linda Detrick.)

Fallen branches, undesirable short-lived trees, and noxious vines overtaking the understory are all reasons for thinning the woods. Thinning lets more light into the understory, allowing desirable hardwoods to sprout and begin the next stage of succession. (Photo by Judi Rutz; © The Taunton Press, Inc.)

Consulting a Forester or Arborist

When thinning a wooded area, use care in selecting which saplings or young trees to remove. If they are part of the next stage of succession, they are probably the good, long-lived trees you want to keep. If you cannot identify them yourself or are unfamiliar with the species of trees typically growing and succeeding in your area, call on the services of your county forester, which should be free of charge, or hire an arborist. Although the decision of who to call may be swayed by economics, be aware of the politics of the two jobs.

A **forester** is trained to manage the woods for the production of pulpwood for making paper or for logging for building materials—in other words, for harvesting trees. His or her bias may not be in keeping with yours or your intentions for the woods. An **arborist** is in the business of saving trees, not cutting them down.

In some larger cities and counties, there are **urban foresters** who are city or state employees and will not charge for their services. This title may be a misnomer because they are doing the job of an arborist by planting and caring for trees on city streets. They are a good source of information if they are available to you. Most are busy just at the time of year you need them, so don't hesitate to seek their advice during their downtime, usually in the dead of winter.

I have watched just such a field in front of my house for several years. The farmer stopped haying it 20 years ago, and now you can't walk between the trees because it has not been managed.

To keep ahead of Mother Nature there are several options you can take, depending on how natural or open you want your wild space to be. To maintain an open field, mow or brushcut annually. For a wooded site, you'll have to decide whether to thin existing trees or clear them completely. After that, a little attention will keep the area in check and make it an asset to your yard.

Thinning and Clearing

Thinning a wooded site allows you to keep the most desirable trees and the benefits they offer your yard, like shade and privacy. Begin the thinning process by marking dead and dying trees. Watch them for a time to see if they are supporting essential wildlife and then decide whether to remove them. Dead trees are often home to wild animals, but they also may be brood wood for insects and plant diseases. The decision to cut or keep trees is a tough one, but I believe that in the long run, the forest will be healthier, safer, and more able to support wildlife if dead and dying trees are removed.

IDENTIFY TREES TO REMOVE AND KEEP

Be sure to observe any covenants there might be on your property concerning the wild areas in case there are restrictions about what can be cut down. Local town offices have this information. Also, establish your property lines and corners prior to cutting to make sure you are indeed cutting or pruning your own trees.

The decision of what healthy trees to remove should be based on your intentions for the woods. If you want to clear a pathway, choose your route and remove the trees that are in your sight line. If you want to plant in the woods, look up at the crowns of the trees and decide which ones will let in the most sunlight. If you want to create a healthier woods, but are impatient about letting it mature on its own, you may just want to remove the first-stage succession trees. When you have identified the small seedlings and saplings and shrubby brush that develops to form the understory of the woods, and you know what you want to remove, you can use a hand saw, lopping shears, and pruners or a chain saw to cut the brush to the ground. This can be trucked away or chipped on site.

If you need more usable yard space, you may decide to clear wooded areas of trees. As in the case of thinning, you need to decide whether you will do the work yourself or call in a professional. If the trees are all saplings and the main problem is brush, you can do the work with a hand saw, lopping shears, and a gasoline-powered brush cutter. Larger trees present a dilemma. Even if you are skilled with a chain saw, tall trees

This tree threatens the house because of its proximity and the direction in which it is leaning. Special care must be taken in its removal to ensure that it won't fall toward the house.
(Photo by Sloan Howard; © The Taunton Press, Inc.)

Tools and Equipment

When working in your yard with various tools and equipment, consider a long-sleeved shirt and long pants, as well as leather work gloves and boots. These will help protect you from most brush-clearing hazards, such as poisonous plants and stinging and biting insects. If you're cutting down trees, a hard hat is a good idea. And if you're using a chain saw or other power equipment such as a chipper/shredder or power brush cutter, wear earmuffs or earplugs for protection. Wear safety goggles to keep woodchips and dust out of your eyes.

A bow saw can be used to cut down small trees and saplings as well as to remove upper branches to make it easier to take down a tree. While you should never stand on a ladder to use a chain saw, it is usually safe to cut branches from a ladder when using handsaws. A pruning saw can also cut moderately thick limbs in small spaces. (Photo by Susan Kahn; © The Taunton Press, Inc.)

Brush cutters have more oomph than weed whips and make the job of removing brush easier than doing it by hand. Brush cutters come in several types. This is a walk-behind type with heavy-duty whipping action. Another effective type is called a Brush Hog, which attaches onto the power take-off of a small tractor. It can be rented from a rental store. (Photo courtesy CHP Marketing Services.)

Heavy-duty lopping shears can prune branches and cut down saplings up to 1½ in. in diameter. For clearing the early stages of brush growth, these shears are invaluable. Hedge shears can also be useful in cutting large areas of fine brush. Bear in mind that these tools will only cut the brush down to the ground, and it will grow back. Regular mowing in brushy areas will be necessary to keep the brush from resprouting. (Photo by Susan Kahn; © The Taunton Press, Inc.)

Use a chipper, available from most rental stores, if you have a pile of branches to dispose of. To chip branches up to 3 in. in diameter or for clearing large areas of brush, you'll need at least a 5-hp engine, but 8 hp or more is preferable. Never exceed the manufacturer's specifications for the branch size or your machine will jam and stall. If you do jam the machine, turn it off and disconnect the lead to the spark plug before attempting to dislodge the stuck material. (Photo by Boyd Hagen; © The Taunton Press, Inc.)

close to a house, power lines, a public road, or other structures pose a tricky proposition. Be frank with yourself about your abilities and don't try anything you don't feel comfortable doing.

TOOLS NEEDED

The tools needed for thinning and clearing are essentially the same tools needed for large-scale pruning (see the photos on the facing page). A few other tools, such as a brush cutter, a chain saw, or a chipper/shredder can be helpful, especially if you have a large area to thin or clear. Check with your local rental center for availability and see if you can share the cost with a neighbor. Of course, always make certain the tools are in good working order and sharpened before you begin.

Taking Down a Tree

Trees smaller than 2 in. in caliper can be removed with a pruning or bow saw, but if you need to remove a tree larger than a sapling, the best tool is a chain saw. If there are several trees close together, cutting can be tricky and dangerous if you aren't trained to know what to anticipate about falling trees and branches. Even trained foresters fall victim to wayward limbs. So my advice is for you to tackle only the small trees easily reached from the ground.

Step 1: Remove all the lower branches you can reach from the ground to clear the stem for cutting. Study the way the tree is standing and decide where the tree should fall. It is easy to hang up a tree on the branches of other trees. If a tree is leaning in a certain direction, your options for where the tree should fall will be limited. You may need to tie a rope on the tree above the halfway point so that it can be pulled in the right direction as it starts to fall (see photo A).

When a tree slated for removal threatens adjacent buildings, a rope must be tied securely to its trunk to aid in pulling and directing the tree away from buildings. (Photo by Sloan Howard; © The Taunton Press, Inc.)

A notch is cut on the side of the tree where it will fall. (Photo by Sloan Howard; © The Taunton Press, Inc.)

A straight cut is made on the other side of the tree toward the notch. (Photo by Sloan Howard; © The Taunton Press, Inc.)

When notched and tied properly, the tree falls away from the house. (Photo by Sloan Howard; © The Taunton Press, Inc.)

Step 2: Assuming the tree is relatively straight and you have a clear space for it to fall, start by cutting a notch on the side of the tree that faces the direction you wish the tree to fall (see photo B on p. 43). Cut the notch at a comfortable cutting height. You can always go back and trim the stump later.

Step 3: When the notch is complete, go to the opposite side of the tree. Begin cutting a second notch opposite and just above the first notch, at an angle toward the first notch (see photo C).

Step 4: As you cut toward the notch, the tree will begin to lean and then fall (see photo D). Often, the tree breaks off before the entire cut is complete. Once the tree is down, trim off the limbs that are small enough to chip. Cut larger limbs for firewood, then cut up the trunk into fireplace lengths for splitting later.

Hiring Tree Professionals

In some cases, it may be necessary to hire a tree service to remove trees and out-of-reach dead branches. If they can get a truck with a lift into the site, they will send a worker up to do pruning in the "cherry picker." If a truck will do too much damage or the site is inaccessible, it may be necessary for the arborist to climb the trees to prune them or to "limb out" trees (i.e., remove all limbs or side branches) for removal.

When trees are standing close to structures, power lines, or roads, or if the trees are very tall (e.g., over 20 ft.), the preferred removal method is to lop off the limbs first and cut down the tree in sections. This takes skill and proper equipment and is best left to the professional. Get estimates from a number of companies and make certain the service you decide on is licensed and insured. Be warned that these services are expensive. One way to make the job more economical is to cut up the tree yourself once it is on the ground and do the clean up.

Dealing with Stumps

After a tree is cut down to the stump, you will need to decide whether to leave the stump in place or to remove it.

Left on its own, a stump will take up to 10 years to decompose fully. If the area will remain wooded or you will underplant with shrubs and perennials, you may elect to leave stumps to rot on their own, hidden by the new plantings. You will need to kill any stumps of trees that were alive when removed; otherwise they may sprout new stems and begin anew. A simple way to do this is to tie black landscape plastic over the stump to keep out sunlight and oxygen and to help prevent the stump from sprouting.

If you want to completely clear an area to make into a lawn, hire a tree service to remove the stumps of large trees that are

Once the branches have been removed and a rope has been secured to the trunk of the tree, an arborist climbs into the tree and cuts off pieces of the tree a few yards at a time. The rope keeps the pieces from straying as they drop.
(Photo by Boyd Hagan; © The Taunton Press, Inc.)

Chain Saw Safety

Follow these guidelines every time you use a chain saw.

• Make sure you are comfortable with the saw and know how to properly use it.

• Make sure the saw weight is light enough for you to control.

• Make sure the anti-kickback bar, hand guard, and tip guard are installed.

• Make sure the chain has been sharpened properly.

• Make sure the chain has been tensioned properly.

• Wear a hard hat and ear protection.

• Only cut a tree that is standing by itself, well away from people and buildings, power lines, and public roads.

• Keep your body out of line with the blade.

• Never use a chain saw above your head or while standing on a ladder.

Very tall trees require the services of a professional arborist for removal. A truck with a cherry picker hoisted this arborist into the tree for easy and safe access to the branches.
(Photo by Boyd Hagan; © The Taunton Press, Inc.)

Removing stumps is quick and safe using a stump grinder. The rotating saw wears away the stump as low into the ground as you want. The remaining roots and main stem can be covered with at least 4 in. of topsoil to support a lawn. (Photo by Boyd Hagan; © The Taunton Press, Inc.)

1 ft. or more in diameter. A stump grinder does it so quickly and easily and with a minimum of damage that it is ludicrous to do it any other way (see photo E).

REMOVING A STUMP

To remove the stumps of smaller (less than 1 ft. in diameter) trees, you will need a sharp ax (or grub hoe), shovel, mattock, and a strong back.

Step 1: Dig around the stump and remove excess soil (see photo F). Then hack away at the roots with the ax or grub hoe until you have cut away the main portion of the stump and left only small roots, 2 in. or less in diameter, in the ground (see photo G).

Step 2: If you have adequately removed all the obstructive roots, you should be able to fill in the hole or leave it in readiness for planting (see photo H). Any residual roots will be small and will not pose a problem because they rot naturally below ground. There are products available at home centers and garden stores that claim to rot away whole stumps, but it takes years for the decomposition to take place, which may not fit your schedule.

If removing a stump by hand, leave some stump for leverage, then shovel away soil surrounding the roots to a distance of a few feet from the main stump. Remove as much soil as possible from the roots before you use a chain saw to cut down on flying debris. (Photo by Sloan Howard; © The Taunton Press, Inc.)

Small feeder roots are chopped easily with an ax. (Photo by Sloan Howard; © The Taunton Press, Inc.)

Fill the hole and cover the area with topsoil. You are now ready to plant new shrubs, trees, and/or lawn. (Photo by Sloan Howard; © The Taunton Press, Inc.)

Eliminating Other Unwanted Plants

After the unwanted trees and brush are gone, the last job in clearing the area is to eliminate vines and weeds, which compete with the healthy plants and may even choke out some trees and shrubs.

USING HERBICIDES

The most effective way to eliminate weeds and undesirable plants, especially those with underground runners such as poison ivy or wild grape vine, is to use a nonresidual, systemic herbicide such as Roundup. Many people are wary of using herbicides to clear unwanted brush and weeds and prefer to do it by hand.

Weeds without underground runners may be pulled by hand and should be if they are mixed in with herbaceous perennials and shrubs leafed to the ground. This is an easier job if it has just rained or if you wet down the area before you begin. Just make sure you pull the entire weed, root and all, out of the ground.

Weeds with underground runners or vining tops that cannot be reached easily are best cleared with an herbicide. The beauty of systemic herbicides is that the whole plant is killed, which is the only way to dispose of these types of weeds. A non-residual herbicide is one that does not remain in the soil, so it is not effective in the elimination of weed seeds. The nonresidual herbicide acts within the system of actively growing plants, moving from the leaves, which it must contact, through the xylem and phloem of the plants to the roots, killing them once and for all. Since it must contact leaves, it is safe to use in the woods around the bases of trees as long as there are

no root suckers with leaves from those trees in the vicinity. It is also safe to use near water systems because it does not reside in the soil.

As I mentioned, for nonresidual herbicide to be effective, the plants must be actively growing, so the air temperature must be between 50°F and 80°F when it is applied. It is applied in spray form and can be purchased ready to use or as a concentrate that you mix and apply with a

Undesirable noxious vines, like this bittersweet vine, must be removed from desirable plants or they will quickly take over. They will spoil the growth habit of the desirable plant, but worse, can strangle and kill it. (Photo by Judi Rutz; © The Taunton Press, Inc.)

Spraying herbicide requires a calm day and dry weather. Drift can be avoided by spraying early in the morning before the sun causes the wind to pick up. The temperature should be between 50°F and 80°F so that weeds are actively growing. Rubber gloves, eye protection, and a rainsuit ensure that the applicator is protected from the chemicals. Here, a backpack sprayer with a hand pump is used. (Photo by Boyd Hagan; © The Taunton Press, Inc.)

watering can or, for large jobs, a backpack sprayer.

To protect against drift to desirable plants, there must be no wind, not even the slightest breeze, when you spray. The best time of day for application is usually very early in the morning. The spray must be allowed to dry on the leaves of the plants, so there must be no rain for at least three hours after application. As a precaution against tracking the herbicide around the yard, I would keep pets and people out of the sprayed area until the spray has dried on the leaves.

It will take 5 to 10 days to see the results. The plants will yellow and wither and can be left to decompose on their own or can be removed. Always use gloves and full clothing when handling plants, like poison ivy, with inherent toxins because the toxins can remain potent even after the plants have died (see "Handling Poison Ivy").

USING BLACK PLASTIC AND WOVEN CLOTH

Plan ahead to keep weeds from reappearing after you've taken the time to eradicate them. Mulching the beds after clearing them will make pulling whole weeds easier because the roots do not hold as fast to the loose mulch. You can discourage weeds in planting beds by using myrify fabric under the mulch. Unlike its predecessor, black plastic, which should not be used in the woods or in any planting bed, myrify fabric is a plastic woven cloth that allows water to seep through but won't allow weeds to grow back up.

There are drawbacks to this miracle product, though. It will take care of existing weeds under the cloth, but not the ones blown in or dropped by birds and animals. Once the roots of these intruders take hold,

---

Handling Poison Ivy

Poison ivy is one of the most common weeds in the country and also the most able to irritate humans. Here's how to handle it safely.

• Always wear protective clothing, such as long-sleeved shirts, pants, and gloves.

• Don't touch exposed skin, other people, or pets with clothing that's been in contact with poison ivy. Pet hair that has rubbed against plants may have ivy oils on them, too. The oils cling to skin and fibers and can be transferred easily.

• Wash all suspect clothing immediately. Do not add to the load any clothing that hasn't come in contact with the poison ivy.

• NEVER burn poison ivy. The irritant can be inhaled through the smoke and affect internal organs.

Weed cloth or woven myrify fabric, while handy in keeping weeds to a minimum, has a dark side as well. It doesn't stop weeds from blowing in and germinating right through the fabric and it often peeks through mulch, resulting in a messy appearance. (Photo by Judi Rutz; © The Taunton Press, Inc.)

they are nearly impossible to pull out of the fabric because of its weave. Also, if a tear occurs in the fabric, existing weeds will grow through the holes. Finally, I find the fabric unsightly when it peeks through mulch that has slid off.

All in all, the safest and most efficient way to kill weeds, roots and all, around trees and shrubs in the woods or in the landscape is with nonresidual, systemic herbicide. It should be a once-or-twice-a-growing-season exercise, and it is quick and thorough.

Once you have begun a management program for the undeveloped areas of your yard, they will only need annual attention. You should continue to manually remove any dead or dying branches and trees. Shrubby plants or vines can be removed with brush-cutting or herbicide. And, as you probably know, weed seeds will sprout regardless of your best efforts, so you will need to use herbicide or to hand-pull the weeds.

5 Reshaping the Land

Before planting a shrub or laying a brick, your first priority should be to examine the level of the soil around the foundation of your house. If the grade, or soil level, is correct, water will drain away from the house properly. If too much settling has occurred, you may be in for a wet basement and foundation damage. Even if you have a dry basement, it's well worth your time to check the grade all around your foundation and the rest of your yard, especially as you make changes to planting beds, patios, walkways, and so on. Every element must be properly pitched to shed water.

Grade is well planned in this landscape. The ground pitches away from the foundation, and a terrace, retained by a stone wall, gently drops the grade another few feet. You can bet there is no water problem in this basement. (Photo © Alan and Linda Detrick.)

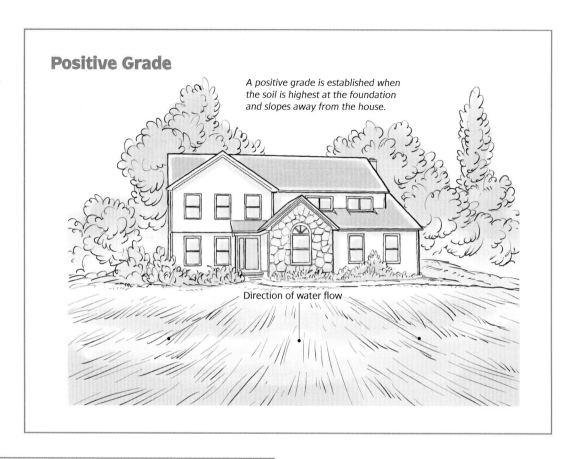

Positive Grade

A positive grade is established when the soil is highest at the foundation and slopes away from the house.

Direction of water flow

Settled Soil

Buried electrical line

It is obvious that an electrical line was buried on the property because the soil on the excavation has settled, resulting in a depression from the street to the meter base on the house. Additional soil is necessary to fill the depression and to disguise the excavation.

In this chapter, you'll learn how to check the grade, improve drainage, and repair your lawn after grade changes are made.

Checking the Grade

Positive grade—where the soil is highest at the house's foundation and slopes away from the house into the yard—should have been established when the house was built. However, this may have changed over the years as the soil around your house settled, especially if any additions have been built onto the house or any ditches have been excavated for electrical, plumbing, or cable lines. If the soil around the foundation or in the excavated areas was not properly compacted when it was spread, air pockets may have gradually worked their way out and caused the soil level to drop in these areas. This can result in negative grade, where the soil level is lower near the foundation,

This sloping yard and landscape ensure that positive grade is maintained near the foundation.
(Photo © Alan and Linda Detrick.)

which allows water to collect and seep into
the house.

It's easiest to check for and correct the
grade if foundation plantings aren't in the
way. If you were planning to move or eliminate some plants near the foundation, now
would be the time to do it. If you are going
to keep all or some of your foundation
plantings, be aware that if you have to add
soil near the foundation to correct the
grade, you'll have to dig up the plants and
replant them. Adding soil on top of a plant's
roots will suffocate it.

To begin evaluating the grade, check the
foundation for cracks, shifting, and settling.
If it is in good shape, but there is water in
the basement, you know that the grade sur-

A level string is attached at the high point of the house and staked at least
8 ft. to 10 ft. perpendicular from the foundation. A line level is attached to
the string to ensure it's level. Use a measuring tape to measure up from the
ground to the string at various intervals. The measurement should increase
as you move away from the house. (Photo by Susan Kahn; © The Taunton Press, Inc.)

A transit is used to establish grade differences. You need a partner to stand at various points in the yard holding a measuring rod. (Photo by Kathleen Kolb.)

rounding the house has problems and should be corrected. This may involve a quick fix of a specific area or adding soil to the entire perimeter of the foundation. If the basement is dry, leave well enough alone and make sure you do not disturb the existing level of soil when you renovate the landscaping close to the foundation.

USING STAKES AND STRING

You can measure the grade using one of two methods. A simple approach involves pounding one stake into the ground at the foundation and another at least 8 ft. to 10 ft. away, perpendicular to the house walls. Run a string between them about 2 ft. off the ground, and place a line level on the string to make sure it is level. Use a yardstick to measure the distance from the ground to the string at the foundation and then, extending outward, do the same at

various intervals until you reach the outside stake. The measurement should become greater as you move away from the house and should be at least 1 in. greater 8 ft. away from the house because water needs a slope of 1 in. in 8 ft. to move. Repeat this procedure around the house foundation to ensure that the grade is positive and needs no adjustment. Your property should drain in a positive direction all the way to the limits of your property.

If you live on sloping property, you may discover that beyond the 8-ft. to 10-ft. distance from the house, farther out in the yard, the grade begins to rise again and that a swale, or gully, keeps water from heading back toward the foundation. This is an adequate way to set up drainage, and it should be left alone.

USING A TRANSIT

For a more high-tech method, you can rent a transit or level to check for positive grade or use a handheld sight level, which you can purchase. With both machines, you must look through the sight to a measuring rod held by a person standing opposite the transit or level. A transit is stationary but pivots to help you accurately check several areas within its range. The person holding the rod will move from spot to spot around the foundation or yard and record onto a map of the yard the measurements you sight through the level. You must establish a baseline measurement, such as the threshold of the house, and then subtract the recorded measurements from the baseline to determine whether the grade is rising or falling. If the measurement is getting larger as you move away from the foundation, you have positive drainage.

An even more sophisticated electronic transit requires less attention at the transit end. A preset measurement is loaded into the transit and, as the measuring rod is adjusted, an intermittent beeping sound is heard. When it has found the right spot, the sound becomes continuous.

Correcting the Grade

If you need to adjust the soil level to correct the grade, you may be able to move the existing soil in your yard, but if you find you need to add large amounts of soil to the foundation or yard, you will have to order it by the truckload. Soil is measured in cubic yards, and a small dump truck holds about 8 to 10 cubic yards of soil. You will probably have to order a full truckload or pick up a smaller amount yourself, although some suppliers will ship less than a full load.

The soil should be of topsoil quality and should be tested before it is purchased (see "Testing the Soil"). It's also important to know the source of the topsoil to be sure it doesn't contain harmful chemicals or contaminants. A routine soil test may not detect certain chemicals such as atrozine, an herbicide used by farmers in their cornfields. It

lasts in soil for at least six years and will inhibit normal plant growth. Sowing a few oat seeds in atrozine-contaminated soil is a good indicator because they are very sensitive to it and will not sprout.

The new topsoil needs to be spread in place to correct the grade. This process is called rough grading. Large amounts of topsoil require the use of heavy machinery, such as a skid-steer loader or bulldozer. Although you can rent a small machine, you may want to hire a professional to do the land-shaping work.

Smaller amounts of soil can be wheelbarrowed into place and spread by hand with a rake. Whether spreading by hand or with a machine, you should be routinely checking the grade with the transit, level, or yardstick as you add soil. The soil will settle, even after you compact it with a roller. To allow for this, adjust your measurements accordingly. Since only 1 in. of grade drop is required in 8 ft. of space, it is not necessary to exaggerate the change in grade, and constant measuring is the only way to detect a change. Also, avoid working any soil when it

Testing the Soil

Before you purchase topsoil, you should have a sample tested to make sure it doesn't contain any harmful chemicals. In addition, as you are digging around the foundation of your house, it's a good idea to perform a soil test. The test will determine what additives are necessary to improve your lawn and the health of your plants. You can buy a test kit at a garden center or send soil samples to the county extension service or soil-testing lab in your state. (There are cooperative extension offices associated with the state universities in every state.)

Take a sample by removing a core of soil from various spots around the yard with a hand trowel. Dig down about 6 in. to 8 in., taking a ½-in. slice of soil. Place the soil

samples together in a bucket and mix them with the trowel. The test kit from the lab will have a bag for this homogeneous sample, which you will fill and send to them. The results you receive from these tests will be more reliable and more comprehensive than a do-it-yourself kit.

It is important to tell the lab what you will be growing in the soil so they can give you the proper recommendations. Simply mention generally whether you are growing lawn or ornamental shrubs, or vegetables or perennials. In about three weeks, you will receive the results, which will indicate the pH (level of acidity) and fertility levels of your soil. With the results, you will be able to properly add lime and fertilizer to correct any deficiencies.

Swale

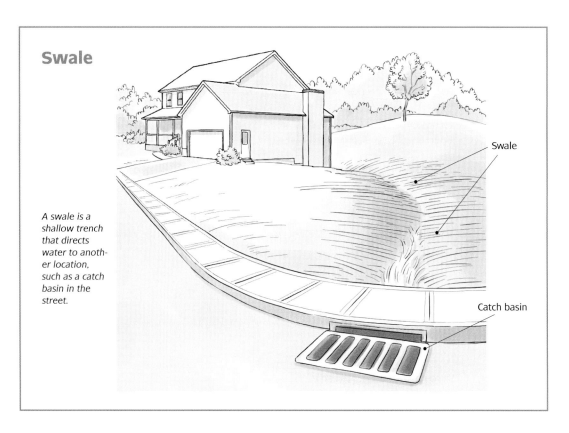

A swale is a shallow trench that directs water to another location, such as a catch basin in the street.

Swale

Catch basin

Dry Well

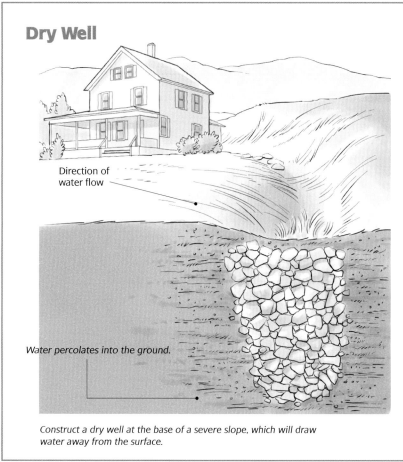

Direction of water flow

Water percolates into the ground.

Construct a dry well at the base of a severe slope, which will draw water away from the surface.

is wet because you will ruin its texture. What was once friable, fluffy soil will become as hard and unworkable as concrete if the texture is ruined.

Creating Drainage Systems

Sometimes, on severely sloped sites or small lots where there is limited distance for water to move, correcting grade isn't enough. Instead, you'll have to create a path and catch area for water drainage.

A swale, which is simply a shallow trench, captures the water and moves it to another part of the yard, to a dry well, or to a subsurface drainage system like a catch basin in the street. A dry well is a pit filled with gravel that draws water and percolates it through the ground. Fortunately, installing these structures isn't quite as complicated as it sounds, but the jobs do require some heavy equipment and a little professional

Installing a Drainage Pipe

If there is a lot of water to move, you can build a subsurface drainage system with a dry well and plastic PVC (polyvinyl chloride) pipe. Water will travel through the pipe and out the holes over the distance of the pipe.

1. Make a dry well as described below. Purchase 4-in.-diameter perforated PVC pipe and fit it with a myrify cloth sock. This will keep silt from plugging the holes.

2. Dig a trench, at least 1 ft. deep and 6 in. wide, from the dry well toward the drainage area. Be sure to drop the level at least 1 in. every 8 ft. for proper drainage.

3. Place 3 in. to 4 in. of washed gravel in the trench, then set in the perforated pipe. Cover with a few more inches of gravel and then topsoil to support a lawn or planting bed.

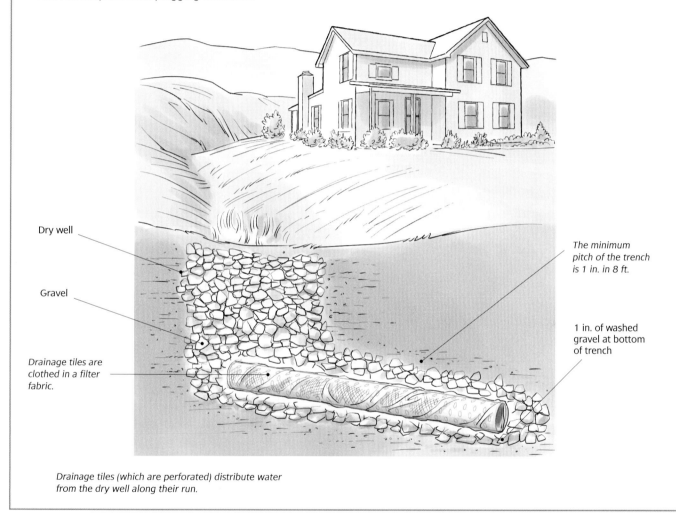

Dry well

Gravel

Drainage tiles are clothed in a filter fabric.

The minimum pitch of the trench is 1 in. in 8 ft.

1 in. of washed gravel at bottom of trench

Drainage tiles (which are perforated) distribute water from the dry well along their run.

know-how. Remember, before digging or excavating anywhere in your yard, notify the local utility companies so they may determine where all the electrical, gas, and water lines are.

An above-ground drainage system, such as a **swale,** should be situated at the base of a slope and should be shallow enough so it doesn't interfere with mowing. It should blend in with the rest of the lawn. If there is not enough distance for the water to dissipate in the swale, it must be directed to a dry well or catch basin.

A **dry well** is created by digging a hole at least 3 ft. deep and 3 ft. wide, lining it with myrify fabric, which will let water in

Dry Well and Solid Pipe

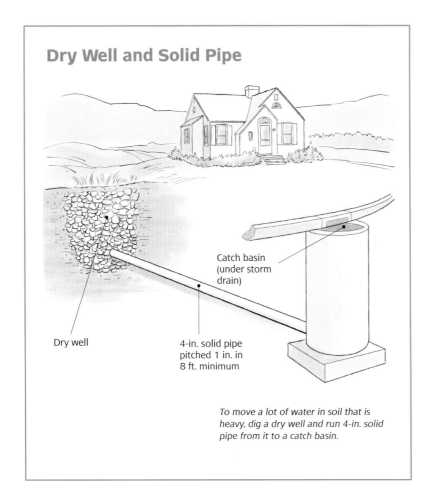

Catch basin (under storm drain)

Dry well

4-in. solid pipe pitched 1 in. in 8 ft. minimum

To move a lot of water in soil that is heavy, dig a dry well and run 4-in. solid pipe from it to a catch basin.

and keep silt out, and filling it with ¾ in. of washed gravel. You may want to put a metal grate on top so your mower will ride over it and not kick up stone, or you can cover the top of the gravel with 4 in. to 5 in. of topsoil and plant grass seed.

If water collects and won't drain properly because the soil is too heavy (as determined by the soil test) or if there is a low spot in the yard where proper grading isn't possible, you may want a pro to install a **catch basin** in the middle of the low spot and dig a trench for a solid pipe to a street catch basin or an area out of harm's way. A catch basin is constructed from a concrete cylinder with a punchout to receive the pipe and a grate on top. In this case, you won't need gravel or myrify fabric in the trench because no water will be leaving the pipe. Be sure the trench is pitched so the water will drain to the outlet.

A lush lawn just begs for bare feet! Whether seeding or sodding, if your lawn is installed properly, it will be a feast for the eyes and a carpet for your feet.
(Photo by Delilah Smittle; © The Taunton Press, Inc.)

Renovating the Lawn

Whether you've made major grade adjustments or just filled in minor depressions, you'll have lawn areas that need to be fixed. This is a good time to take a look around your yard to see if there are other bare spots or sparse areas that need attention. Renovating the lawn can be done by either seeding or laying sod.

SEEDING

Adding soil to an already established lawn is called topdressing, and it is a common practice (see photo A). Topsoil is added to the depressions no matter how large, right on top of the existing lawn, and it is raked smooth to blend with the main level of the lawn. Soil amendments are then raked in with new grass seed. Here's how.

Step 1: For a large damaged area, place 3 in. to 4 in. of topsoil over a well-graded base of soil. Rake out the topsoil to remove all rocks and roots. For grassy areas that need repairs, start by mowing the existing lawn to a height of about 2 in. Then spread about 2 in. of topsoil right over the lawn and rake it to lawn level.

Step 2: Distribute fertilizer and lime with a cyclone spreader (see photo B). This provides the best coverage and avoids the striped look a drop spreader creates. Fertilize and lime in two directions to make sure you have good coverage.

Step 3: Seed the lawn with the cyclone spreader. Use a grass seed mixture with 10 percent to 15 percent annual rye for quick germination, with the rest a mixture of perennial rye and fescues, both creeping and tall. So-called "quick cover" grass is all annual rye and will die with the first frost, but a small amount of annual rye in the mix

A grading rake is used to sift debris, such as rocks and weeds, from freshly spread topsoil. It works like a fine-toothed comb. (Photo by Boyd Hagan; © The Taunton Press, Inc.)

A

B

Adding soil to an existing lawn is called topdressing. Topdress to fill minor depressions and sparse areas. Seed right over the existing areas and, in no time, the new lawn will blend with the old. (Photo by Boyd Hagan; © The Taunton Press, Inc.)

A cyclone spreader distributes fertilizer, lime, and seed over a broad area. (Photo by Boyd Hagan; © The Taunton Press, Inc.)

A newly seeded lawn is covered with salt marsh hay to protect the seed from erosion, hold in moisture, and shade the tiny grass plants as they germinate. (Photo by Boyd Hagan; © The Taunton Press, Inc.)

controls erosion and shades the ground while the other grasses germinate.

Step 4: Spread sterile straw or salt marsh hay over your newly seeded lawn. Just a light coating is all that's needed to conserve moisture (see photo C). If it's too thick, the grass will struggle to get through and will not receive enough sunlight.

Step 5: Water, water, water. In order for germination to take place, the top 2 in. of soil must be kept moist.

Step 6: Mow as soon as the grass needs it. Mowing encourages side branching and root growth, which are needed for a successful lawn.

SODDING

For instant gratification, sodding a lawn is the way to go, especially if you have small areas to repair (it's expensive to do large areas). The base preparation is the same as for seeding (see steps 1 and 2 on p. 59). Sod must be handled carefully. It should be delivered on the day you intend to lay it, and you shouldn't order more than you can lay on that day. Sod is harvested on the day you lay it because it doesn't have a shelf life. Here are the basic steps.

Step 1: When the pallet of rolled-up sod arrives, place it in the shade and get started (see photo D). Do not water it—it will be difficult to work with.

Step 2: Move a few rolls to the area you are working in. Unroll the first piece in place, starting at one of the top corners, where you will not be leaning on it as you add pieces. Get down on your hands and knees. Rubber knee pads are helpful.

Made for the Shade

If there are areas of your lawn that are patchy because of too much shade (moss is a telltale sign), you should consider removing the lawn and planting shade-loving ground covers or making a planting bed in that space. Often these areas have a too-low pH, which makes the soil acidic due to a buildup of leaves from surrounding trees.

Separate soil samples should be taken to determine the pH of these patchy areas. If the pH is below 6.0, it will be a losing battle to grow lawn, no matter how much lime you add. My suggestion would be to plant acid soil–loving plants, such as rhododendrons and hollies or ground covers like lowbush blueberries, and stop fighting the forces of nature.

Rolled-up sod arrives on pallets. It should be used the day it arrives and stored in the shade until you are ready for it. (Photo by Sloan Howard; © The Taunton Press, Inc.)

E

F

Knit the sod joints together, leaving a little slack for complete contact between pieces. Do not overlap them, though. (Photo by Sloan Howard; © The Taunton Press, Inc.)

A garden hose is a handy guide when cutting sod on a curve. (Photo by Sloan Howard; © The Taunton Press, Inc.)

Step 3: Butt the new piece of sod up against the existing lawn, which should have been cut to a straight edge to make a smooth seam (see photo E). Leave no space between. If you leave slack in the piece of sod, it is easier to make sure both pieces have complete contact, but do not overlap the piece. Continue to knit pieces together, staggering the joints.

Step 4: When you meet the edge of a planting bed, leave extra sod overlapping the edge of the bed and use a sod knife or spade to cut the sod to follow the edge of the bed. A garden hose can be used as a prop to shape the bed if the edges of the bed have not been cut yet (see photo F).

Step 5: At the edge of walkways, driveway, and beds, push soil up over the edges of the sod to keep roots from drying out (see photo G).

Step 6: When the laying job is finished, roll the sod with a water-filled drum roller so the sod makes complete contact with the soil beneath (see photo H).

Step 7: Water the sod generously every day to generate root growth. Keep people and pets off the sod until you see top growth. As soon as it needs mowing, do so. At that point, it is ready to walk on.

G

H

Soil must cover all exposed ends of the sod so it won't dry out. A rake is used to push the soil against the open ends. (Photo by Sloan Howard; © The Taunton Press, Inc.)

The final procedure before watering is rolling the sod with a drum roller to ensure good contact with the soil beneath. (Photo by Sloan Howard; © The Taunton Press, Inc.)

6 Reshaping the Planting Beds

Once the grade problems have been corrected or added to your checklist for action, you are ready to reshape the planting beds to accommodate any new plants and enhance the locations of old ones. When reshaping beds, keep in mind that geometric shapes are generally not as pleasing as curves, which are more in keeping with nature's shapes.

Shaping the planting beds is a simple procedure that often is the tell-tale sign of a professional job. You can achieve professional results by following nature's curves and making deep, definitive edges. (Photo by Sloan Howard; © The Taunton Press, Inc.)

A layered planting uses large shrubs and trees in the background, medium-sized shrubs and taller perennials in the middle, and low, ground-hugging shrubs and perennials in the front. Note the texture and color mix, which adds interest to the planting. (Photo by Dency Kane.)

It's not difficult to make curved beds out of straight ones—simply use a garden hose to outline the shape. Be generous in the sweep of the curves because too many ins and outs look contrived and do not mimic nature. And don't scrimp on width. Many older homes have one line of shrubbery across the front of the house with a 4-ft.-wide straight bed. Even in the most formal plantings today, landscape designers try to layer the plantings so that different-sized plants grow in front of each other, with the tallest in the rear and ground covers and perennials colorfully skirting the front of the bed.

Plan before You Cut

Before you reshape your planting beds, plan it all out on paper. To do this, you will have

to make decisions about what you will keep, what will be moved to other areas of the yard, and what will be discarded (see Chapter 2, beginning on p. 16). A low-maintenance foundation planting will use

---

SIZING THE BED

The wider the bed, the more interesting layers you can plant. I recommend a bed at least 7 ft. to 8 ft. wide at the corners of the house where a taller shrub will anchor the planting, tapering in to 4 ft. or 5 ft. wide at the first nook and widening out to 5 ft. or 6 ft. where it meets the walkway.

A multidimensional layered planting is enhanced by a backdrop of climbing roses and window boxes filled with annuals, graduating down to very low-growing ground covers tumbling onto the walkway. (Photo by Steve Silk; © The Taunton Press, Inc.)

base plants that ultimately reach no taller than 4 ft. to 6 ft., depending on the height of your house windows from the ground.

You can keep plants that meet those specifications with or without pruning, but understand that if you decide to keep a plant that really wants to be 10 ft. tall, it will be a never-ending battle to keep it smaller. The middle layer of plants should grow to 2 ft. or 3 ft. and will be used to cover the stems of the base plants as well as to provide accents of color and texture for the whole garden. The front layer will be short and spreading, with ground covers and perennials planted in groupings.

PROPORTION AND SCALE

When you are planning the planting beds (or a walkway or patio) you must consider proportion and scale in your design. Presumably, the reason for renovating in the first place has something to do with scale, such as when the plants have overgrown their space or the manicured portion of the yard is more than you can manage. By using plants that stay compact in maturity, you will reduce your maintenance and enhance the features of your home with plants that complement it, not overtake it.

When you consider the size of the front stoop and walkway, you will balance space needs and safety with good design. Two people can walk comfortably side by side on a 4-ft.-wide walkway, and it is probably still in scale to be a little more generous, but you would not want to go so wide that the walkway becomes the focal point of the yard. Conversely, any width much less than 4 ft. for a front walkway looks and feels ridiculously narrow.

If you don't already have the information in your plant diary on the plants you want to

An in-scale walkway balances space needs and safety with good design. Two people can walk comfortably side-by-side on a walkway about 4 ft. wide. (Photo by Chris Curless; © The Taunton Press, Inc.)

include in your reshaped beds, you will need to research their ultimate heights and spreads so the spacing within the beds will be adequate for the long run. The planting may look a little sparse in the beginning, but when it fills in, each plant should have the right amount of space. If you want a group of plants to grow together to eventually look like one plant, you can place those plants closer together from the start.

You may decide to include a specimen plant, which will provide a focal point and most likely be taller than the base plants. This may be a small vase-shaped or weeping flowering tree, which will need space to spread its branches. Often a special curve is incorporated into the bed to accommodate the specimen plant.

EXPOSURE AND HARDINESS

You will also need to consider exposure when keeping and choosing plants. Many plants are particular about sun and shade and how much of each they will tolerate.

Determine the compass reading of the side of the house you are designing in order to choose the correct plants. An existing plant may not be doing well because it may need more sun or shade or it may be shaded by plants near it, causing it to be misshapen or sparsely leaved or flowered.

Generally speaking, a plant living on the east side of the house receiving morning sun should be tolerant of partial shade, as should a plant on the west side that receives only afternoon sun. Shade plants prefer the northern side of the house. A southerly exposure is the harshest because not only does a plant get blasted by sun all summer, but the winter sun and winds will desiccate and burn it if it is not properly protected or does not inherently tolerate a southern exposure. Of course, there are many factors that can alter direct exposure, among them trees, buildings, and windscreens, so don't overlook them when taking your compass readings.

Consider the hardiness of your plants. If the existing plants are thriving, they are happy in your climate. Any additional plants will have to be chosen with hardiness in mind. Your garden center should carry only plants that will successfully live in your area, but sometimes it will carry plants that are marginally hardy

WATER IN YOUR NEIGHBORHOOD?

If there is a body of water nearby, it can affect the planting zone in your yard by creating milder temperatures, longer or shorter seasons, higher winds, and higher humidity. Before choosing plants, discuss hardiness with fellow gardeners in the neighborhood to get some idea of what you can expect.

and require winter protection or a special microclimate, such as the inside corner of a house where it will be warmer and less windy.

If you are interested in a low-maintenance landscape, think carefully before purchasing a marginally hardy plant. It will require more maintenance because it will need to be wrapped and mulched for winter, and it may even require you to plant a windscreen to lessen the exposure it will receive. If you do not take precautions, the plant will die back in some winters and need careful pruning and fertilizing to revitalize it. And if a plant often looks half-dead, it is not an asset to your garden or landscape.

COLOR AND TEXTURE

Don't lock yourself in to the same colors and textures you've always had. The best designers try to include a mix of plants showing color and interest in every season. Evergreens provide color and texture all the time. Flowering shrubs bloom at different times during the growing season, may have good fall color or persistent berries, and may have interesting twig structure for sculptural interest in the winter garden. Some perennials and ground covers are evergreen, but

some die back completely, leaving spaces in the winter, so it is important that the base plants provide color at that time of year.

Consider all the attributes of the plant when you are making choices. It is a bonus when the same plant can contribute more than one season of interest to a planting.

Texture is the hardest concept to understand. One aspect of texture involves shape relationships, such as a combination of tall, spiky plants with horizontally branched spreaders. A good example is a clump of foxgloves planted next to daisylike gaillardia. They are both herbaceous perennials, but the spiked flower heads of the foxgloves contrast in texture and shape with the flat, rounded flower heads of the gaillardia.

Plant Buyer's Checklist

Before heading off to the garden center to purchase your new plants, you need to know the exposure in the planting areas (full sun, shade, or partial shade), as well as the characteristics of your existing plants and the blooming period and/or season of interest missing from the planting areas. Use the following checklist to help determine what characteristics you should be looking for in your new plants.

❏ Plant(s) with autumn interest—fall color or berries

❏ Plant(s) with spring interest—flowers

❏ Plant(s) with summer interest—flowers or interesting foliage

❏ Plant(s) with winter interest—berries, sculptural interest, or colorful bark

❏ Early, midseason, or late bloom time

❏ Plants that are upright, spreading, or weeping

❏ Size and spread of plant(s) at maturity

❏ Evergreen or deciduous plants

Changes in texture make a planting bed more interesting. Here, grasses and ferny-leaved coreopsis, narrow-leaved daylilies, succulent-leaved sedum, and broad-leaved shrubs all contribute to texture variations. (Photo by Boyd Hagan; © The Taunton Press, Inc.)

Texture is also the way you think a plant feels without touching it, feeling it through your eyes. The goal is to achieve a mix of textures, such as an evergreen yew planted with a broadleaved evergreen like a rhododendron. Both will provide cover year-round and can be used as base plants, and they are much more interesting together than using two of the same plant.

BALANCE

Balance is another design consideration when planning a landscape. Many people are most comfortable with a symmetrical planting in which the same and equal number of plants match on both sides. In some situations, like the foundation planting of a very formal Georgian house, this is a good approach, but it isn't the only approach. One tall plant with the same or heavier texture can balance three shorter plants in an asymmetrical arrangement on both sides of an entry.

Asymmetrical balance is also achieved through the creative use of color and texture. Designers call this repetition, which is important to incorporate in the planting so your eye is drawn across the whole picture.

For instance, red can be repeated from one end of the planting to the other but still not be derived from the same plants.

Picture a planting area that contains a base shrub that has red flowers in the summer planted to the left. A middle-layer plant or group of plants with red-colored leaves are planted to the left of center. A shrub with red berries is planted to the right of center, and another plant that flowers in summer with red flowers is to the far right. The picture is completed with a continuum of intermittent red leaves and flowers bordering the front of the planting.

OUTLYING BEDS AND SPECIALTY GARDENS

As you plan to move plants that have grown too large to other beds in the yard, think about creating planting beds for definition and screening, and as transition from cultivated to wild space. The added bonus is that these plants will help to screen out the neighbors, noise, and wind.

If you have enough of the same plant, you can make a hedge. More likely, you will have a mix of plants with which to work, which lends itself well to an informal

Silver foliage and white flowers are a few of the repetition tricks used in this bed to draw your eyes across the whole planting. (Photo © Alan and Linda Detrick.)

The plantings are not identical on both sides of this fence opening, yet they are balanced. (Photo by Boyd Hagan; © The Taunton Press, Inc.)

arrangement—again, placing the taller plants to the rear of a layered planting, rather than just lining them up in a row. Such an arrangement is aesthetically pleasing and also more effective as a screen because, when you offset the plants in front of each other and alternate them, you fill the gaps in the planting. Don't be afraid to mix evergreen with deciduous—it will be a more natural-looking planting and offer interest throughout the seasons.

When you plan the shape of outlying beds, you can be just as creative as for the beds near the house. Long sweeping curves that follow the arrangement of the plants in the bed will be interesting from a distance and will blend well with any contours existing in the yard. Fencing can be added as a backdrop or divider between properties or as a divider between cultivated and uncultivated areas.

> ### PLANNING FOR CHANGE
> Before moving plans, make sure they are suitable for their new environment. Keep in mind that they are losing the protection of the foundation, which has afforded them warmth and windscreening over the years, and that shade-loving plants that were growing on the north or east side of the house may not thrive in an open, sunny location in the side yard.

Naturally shaped island beds, where you can walk around the entire bed and see the plantings, are often used as focal points or accents or to hide an unsightly feature, such as a wellhead or septic clean-out in the

Side Yard Planting

A side yard planting of mixed deciduous and evergreen plants creates definition between yards and provides privacy and wind screening.

An island planting bed makes an excellent focal point in the yard, especially if it's used to hide an unsightly feature like a well-head. The plants graduate down in size from the middle to the edges. (Photo by Chris Curless; © The Taunton Press, Inc.)

yard. Free-form shapes or more familiar kidney shapes work well. In island beds, the tallest plants are located in the middle and the layers graduate down to the borders.

Backyard plantings should be planned according to how your family uses the yard and the flow patterns of people and pets. It is nearly impossible to change the habits of a pet, so locate plantings where they will not be in the pathway of dog to door. Use plantings to direct people by creating beds where you don't want traffic. Place the new routes so people don't have to go way out of their way to avoid the beds.

Plantings can be used to separate spaces and make privacy. For instance, a quiet garden nook for reading or dozing can be separated from the main play area of the yard with carefully placed and selected plantings.

You can move specialty plantings, such as vegetable and herb gardens, especially if you expand a patio or deck and the expansion interferes with their present location. However, unless you are willing to start over, if you have spent years building up the soil in the vegetable garden or you grow hard-to-transplant perennial vegetables like aspara-

Herbs are beautifully integrated into this landscape planting instead of segregated to another part of the yard. (Photo by Delilah Smittle; © The Taunton Press, Inc.)

gus and rhubarb, you may consider this garden a permanent one to build around.

An herb garden can be easily transplanted to another site with only a slight setback in production. The renovation may offer the opportunity to change the shape of the herb garden, elaborate on its planting scheme, or introduce new plants to the garden. Moving herbs or other perennials is actually a healthy practice because they may badly need dividing. Not only will the plants benefit from the division, but you will multiply your supply for use elsewhere in the yard.

Other specialty gardens may be planned for the yard at this time. Water gardens, small fruit plantings or orchards, wildflower gardens, and perennial borders are a few examples of gardens you can design. If you have a sculpture or gazebo, or plan to add one in the future, you may want to plan a garden around these features. A pool or spa will need to be landscaped, and a whole area of the yard will need to be planned around these major additions, which may

include fencing, a shed for the pool equipment or changing, and plantings (see Chapter 12, beginning on p. 150).

CONSULT YOUR DIARY

After you have finished sketching your design, refer to the list of keeper plants in your diary and try to match up the plants you have cataloged with the circles you have designated on the tracing paper. Of course, take all factors into account: mature size, bloom time, color, exposure requirements, and so on. Where your existing plants fit the criteria of the new design, designate them on the plan.

You may want to explore possibilities for reshaping the front walkway, stoop, or patio. In that case, the plan for the planting beds should be put on hold until after you have designed those changes. That way, the shapes you draw will enhance the new shapes of the hardscaping and work in concert with them for a cohesive plan.

Cutting the Beds

If the lawn is established along the front of the house, the new layout for your beds can be carved right out of the lawn area, and the finished bed will look like it has always been there. If the original bed is wider in places, you should try to save some of the sod you are removing to fill in the new nooks.

Step 1: Lay out the new shape of the beds with a garden hose (see photo A). Be sure to give a generous curve.

A hose weaving in and out of the existing straight bed shows the intended new shape. (Photo by Sloan Howard; © The Taunton Press, Inc.)

The sod is pieced in and the joints are knitted together. Now grass is needed to complete the shape. (Photo by Sloan Howard; © The Taunton Press, Inc.)

The new shape is complete. Sod has been removed and replaced to create a serpentine bed. (Photo by Sloan Howard; © The Taunton Press, Inc.)

Sod is cut and lifted to be reused in the new shaping of the bed. The sod is divided into manageable sizes for moving and reestablishing. (Photo by Sloan Howard; © The Taunton Press, Inc.)

Step 2: With a sharp, flat shovel, carefully cut under the existing lawn in strips wide enough to fit the gaps, taking roots and some soil (about 3 in. of material in all) with it (see photos B and C). Trim the grass you are meeting with the sod pieces so it is straight, not ragged. That way you are assured of a good weave. If the gap you are filling is small, try to make the sod piece the same shape. If it is large, make strips in straight pieces and fit them side by side to

fill the gap. You'll have to leave a little slack to knit the pieces together. Always cover any edges with soil that don't meet existing lawn, so the ends will not dry out. Those will be the edges that face into the planting bed—all others should meet the existing lawn perfectly (see photo D on p. 73).

Planting the Beds

Once your beds have been reshaped and dug up, get them ready for planting by clearing out all weeds, surface rocks, and grass. Do any necessary grading, then rake.

Whether you are transplanting from other beds or setting in new plants, spend some time arranging the plants on the ground before you start digging. Don't feel you are locked in to what you sketched on your plan if you find that a plant looks better in another location within the bed. Just keep that plant's requirements in mind and be sure to put it in the right exposure and give it the space it needs to grow.

A landscape plan shouldn't be taken literally like an architectural blueprint. You are dealing with living things that change size and shape, unlike wood and brick buildings. Be sure to leave plenty of space between plants for that growth. This is where the

The design of this mature perennial bed took into account spacing, texture, and color. Remember, you are dealing with living things that change size and shape with maturity, so plan accordingly. (Photo © Brian Vanden Brink.)

Give Beds the Perfect Edge

The edge of the beds can make the difference between a professional-looking job and an amateur one. If you are making a curved bed, be sure it is just that—there should be no flat areas that spoil the curve. By the same token, if you are making a straight bed, run a string between stakes placed at equal distance from the house to use as a guide, so the bed will be perfectly straight and equal in width.

To ensure a good, clean cut, I use a flat, straight spade or an edging tool. The edging tool is rounded and sometimes has a lip to stop the edger from digging too deeply. I like a deep edge to create real definition between lawn and planting bed, while still leaving about 2 in. to 3 in. for mulch.

Place plants where they will be planted. Draw a circle with the shovel to mark the exact spots. (Photo by Sloan Howard; © The Taunton Press, Inc.)

notes in your plant diary come in handy. All that research you did earlier will pay off in well-designed beds. Don't fret about the sparse look of your beds in the beginning. Five years from now, when the plants are mature, the planting bed will look perfect.

When you have all the plants placed where you want them, it's time to plant.

Step 1: Use your shovel to mark the ground around the ball or container and move the plant out of the way (see photo E).

Step 2: Measure the root ball with your shovel while the plant is still wrapped with burlap or in the container to determine how deep to make the hole (see photo F). Do not plant any deeper than where the soil ends now on the shrub or tree stem. If you bury the plant deeper, it will suffocate.

Step 3: Make the planting hole at least 6 in. wider than the root ball all the way around (see photo G). Dig a square-sided hole, not one that is U-shaped. Remove any

Measure the root ball with the shovel head to make sure the depth of the hole will be no deeper than where the soil ends on the stem in the container. (Photo by Sloan Howard; © The Taunton Press, Inc.)

Compare the measurement of the root ball to the depth of the hole. (Photo by Sloan Howard; © The Taunton Press, Inc.)

Dig the hole wider than the root ball, but no deeper. Stomp the soil in the bottom of the hole to remove root-drying air pockets. (Photo by Sloan Howard; © The Taunton Press, Inc.)

Place the plant in the hole (minus its container) with its best face outward. Then backfill the hole with soil. (Photo by Sloan Howard; © The Taunton Press, Inc.)

Stomp the backfilled soil around the entire plant with your heel to remove air pockets. (Photo by Sloan Howard; © The Taunton Press, Inc.)

Rake a dam around the plant to hold water. Soak the plant immediately after planting, and monitor for moisture throughout the growing season. (Photo by Sloan Howard; © The Taunton Press, Inc.)

obstructions in the hole, such as rocks and roots. Roots can be pruned away at both ends with pruners or loppers.

Keep checking the depth as you dig. You can do this by measuring the shovel against the root ball of the plant and then against the depth of the hole you have dug. If you dig a little deeper than you should have, put soil back in and stomp on it to compress and remove air pockets (see photo H on p. 75).

Step 4: Remove all coverings from the plant: burlap, wire basket, or container. If the root ball is falling apart, keep the burlap on the ball, but untie it and tuck it down around the ball after the plant is in the hole. You can only leave the burlap in the hole if it is the kind that disintegrates. The type that doesn't disintegrate is usually green and sometimes plastic.

Step 5: Position the plant so that its best side is facing the way you see it most (see photo I). Then backfill the hole with soil.

Step 6: Backfill in stages and remove any rocks as you go along. Throw in about a third of the soil and stomp around the root ball (see photo J). Throw in the next third and stomp again. Put the final amount into the hole, and stomp again.

Step 7: Make a ring about 4 in. to 6 in. wider than the ball for a dam to hold water. Water immediately and thoroughly, filling the dam several times (see photo K).

Step 8: As soon as all the plants are planted and watered, rake out the bed, leaving shallow dams around the plants (see photo L). Grade the bed so that it is pitched away from the house.

If you haven't done so already, shape the edges of the bed with good depth, about 4 in. or 5 in. at the edge.

When all the plants have been planted, rake out and grade the entire bed, allowing for positive pitch. Leave shallow dams around the plants to catch water, and edge the bed to create a distinction between the lawn and planting bed. (Photo by Sloan Howard; © The Taunton Press, Inc.)

Step 9: Mulch with shredded bark (use softwood or hardwood, whichever is customary for your region) to a depth of 2 in. to 3 in. In this case, more is not better because mulch will suffocate plants just like soil. Use just enough to be effective, and do not use nuggets or stone because they do not hold in moisture or insulate the ground like shredded bark.

Step 10: Any tree—taller than 5 ft. for evergreen and larger than 1½-in. caliper for deciduous—should be staked at this point (see Chapter 8, beginning on p. 94). Smaller trees planted in heavy prevailing winds should be staked as well.

7 Pruning Simplified

If you can't see the front door of your house or if the once-sunny front room has become as dark as a cave, your plants may be in dire need of pruning. This is the simplest form of landscape renovation, and it achieves dramatic results if done properly. However, don't dive into the task without the know-how because you can do serious damage to plants if you prune with the wrong tools, at the wrong time, or with the wrong technique or if you prune the wrong parts of plants.

Shade, mildew, and dangerously leaning trees are just a few consequences of a house built in the middle of the woods. Pruning is usually the best way to remedy these problems without removing the plants entirely. (Photo by Jerry Markatos.)

Overgrown foundation plantings block windows and appear way out of scale, dwarfing the house. (Photo by Ken Druse, garden design by William Wallis Associates.)

Prune for Healthy Plants

There are several reasons for pruning. First, pruning not only makes a plant smaller, but it also can improve or initiate flowering if it has been sparse. By pruning off growing tips that would have become more branches and leaves, the plant's energy is spent on the remaining twigs and branches, which causes the plant to grow vigorously and activates flowering. Second, pruning shapes plants, even if it is minimal. Informal shaping may involve plucking a few wayward twigs here and there, while more formal shaping creates close-clipped hedges and specialty forms like topiary and espalier.

Another important reason for pruning is that it improves the overall health of a plant that has been neglected and left to its own devices. A shrub with a tangled mass of vegetation has poor air circulation, which creates a nice, moist home for diseases and insects. Already dead or dying sections invite insects and disease to breed and should be removed immediately.

Consult your plant diary and plant encyclopedia to determine plant habits, so your pruning will be in keeping with the natural tendencies of the plants. In other words, if a plant wants to weep, do not cut off its trailing branches, or it will be a never-ending battle and the plant will never look right.

Tools of the Trade

Good, clean pruning cuts allow plants to get back into the business of growing without too much recovery time. The only way to make clean cuts is with the right (sharp) tools and proper techniques. There are three major problems you want to avoid when pruning shrubs and trees. One is smashing the twig or branch as you try to remove a part of it. Another is peeling bark down a tree or shrub because your cut did not release completely. The third is injuring other twigs and branches while you are pruning their neighbors. A plant needs to heal those wounds before it can continue to grow, and that is a real setback to the plant.

Almost all the pruning you'll do, from cutting back perennials to removing small tree limbs, can be done with a few simple tools. The first, and one you will use most, is **hand pruners.** There are two types, anvil and bypass. Bypass, or scissors-type, pruners are preferred by most gardeners and professionals. You risk smashing branches with anvil pruners, while the bypass always makes a good, clean cut with little strain on your hands.

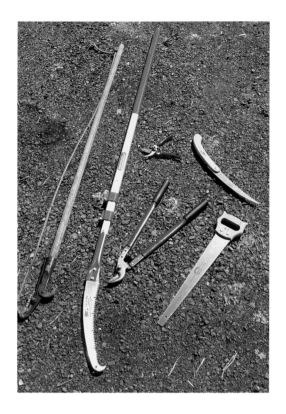

An array of pruning tools from left to right: pole pruner, pole saw, bypass hand pruners, bypass loppers, folding bow saw, straight pruning saw.
(Photo by Boyd Hagan; © The Taunton Press, Inc.)

A good set of **bypass pruners** is expensive, but worth it. They will last forever if you keep them clean and dry, and you can change the blades when they lose their edge. A sharp pair of pruners will remove a branch up to ½ in. in diameter without too much effort. Any larger (up to 1½ in. in diameter) and you are moving into lopper range.

Take Good Care of Your Tools

Pruning tools will last for years if cared for and stored properly. They should be wiped down after use to clean them and prevent rusting. You may have to use a solvent to remove sap from blades, and you should oil moving parts and bolts to keep them in action.

The tools must be kept sharp to make clean, quick cuts. Use a whetstone to sharpen the blades of bypass pruners, loppers, and hedge shears. Only the outside edge of both blades should be sharpened, and your whetstone should be kept oiled during the sharpening. Do not attempt to change the existing angle of the blades. Use a file to remove nicks in the blades.

Good bypass hand pruners have replaceable blades, which are easy to change. Most pruning saws have replaceable blades that just snap in or are easily changed by loosening a few bolts. I always keep extra blades on hand for large jobs.

There are probably many of you chain-saw pruners reading this and wondering, "Why all the handwork?" The ungainliness of a chain saw coupled with the danger of using it in positions it shouldn't be used in make it a tool suited only to cutting down whole trees or huge tree limbs you can reach from the ground. Without fail, whenever I have tried to prune out a large stem from a live shrub with a chain saw, I have nicked and shredded adjacent stems, which I had no intention of pruning out.

It's easy enough to nick with a hand saw, but at least you have more control and can stop in time if you are close to harming another shrub part.

Remember, once you damage a plant, the plant must then put its energy into healing rather than growing, and that takes time and puts undue stress on the plant.

Bypass loppers are enlarged pruners with handles about 2 ft. long. It makes no difference whether the handles are wooden or aluminum as long as the entire tool is heavy duty. Do not purchase the cheapest pair you can find because they will not last; I've had a cheap aluminum pair literally fold up in my hands as I was using them. Look for padded handles, which can make a big difference for your hands.

The next essential pruning tool is the **pruning saw,** which differs from a carpentry saw in that it is designed to cut green wood. The teeth are shaped to resist gumming, and the shape of the tool allows access to tough angles and small spaces. Some pruning saws look much like carpentry saws, while others have curved blades that fold into the handle for safe transport and storage. Another, called a bow saw, has a straight, narrow blade with a curved handle for gripping. It looks a lot like a coping saw for carpentry.

The type of pruning saw you choose to use is really a matter of personal preference. For hard-to-reach high branches, a pole pruner extends the saw on a long, usually telescoping, handle. Many have a lopper tool as well, which is controlled by a squeeze handle or rope near your hands.

Pruning shears are handy for evergreen trees, shrubs, and hedges. They have a bypass mechanism with long blades and handles. Padded, shock-absorbing handles are worth the price because the repetitive action of opening and closing the blades over a long period of time will do a job on your hands. Electric and gas-powered hedge shears are available for rental, but take care not to sever the cord of the electric variety and your limbs and fingers with either one. These are dangerous tools even if you've had lots of experience with them.

Time It Right

Successfully pruning evergreen and deciduous shrubs and trees owes as much to timing as it does to knowing how and where to make the cut. If you prune a plant at the wrong time of year, you risk removing flower buds or causing severe dieback or death.

PRUNE WITH CARE

When you prune a plant you are essentially wounding it. Because diseases can be easily carried from wound to wound, it is important that you disinfect your tool blades as you move from plant to plant or, at the least, from species to species. Carry a cloth and spray bottle of rubbing alcohol along with your tools so you can disinfect the tool blades with the alcohol. A carpenter's tool belt is handy for carrying a variety of tools, including your cloth and spray bottle.

In four-season climates, *never* prune any plant, evergreen or deciduous, when it is getting ready to go into dormancy for the winter. As I have already mentioned, pruning stimulates growth, and if you stimulate growth when the plant is going into dormancy, the new, green growth won't survive the winter. Those soft parts will die back, and young plants may never recover. A plant generally spends the late summer and autumn months "hardening off" in preparation for winter. A good rule of thumb is to *suspend all pruning from late summer until after the plant is dormant*—usually early winter. Once the plant is dormant, you can prune all you want without injuring the plant—it will not be stimulated into growth until the days get longer and the temperatures get warmer. This goes for deciduous shrubs and trees that bloom on the current season's wood.

Your plant encyclopedia or diary will tell you when your plants bloom, and if it is after the spring, the flower buds do not form until the plant starts growing during the current growing season. You will not affect the flower buds by pruning them dur-

ing the winter months or early in the spring. In fact, best flowering will be on new, vital wood, and by pruning, you will stimulate that growth.

There is one exception to pruning during the winter: Deciduous plants that bloom

This overgrown lilac (center of photo) shows tall spindly branches reaching for the sky. Suckering branches have been removed, and the old spindly ones have been left. This is just the opposite of the proper pruning of deciduous shrubs.
(Photo by Sloan Howard; © The Taunton Press, Inc.)

The lilac shrub has been rejuvenated. Old, thick stems were removed, leaving young, vital shoots, which produce flowers in abundance.
(Photo by Sloan Howard; © The Taunton Press, Inc.)

A shriveled and darkened branch indicates deadwood that must be pruned. (Photo by Boyd Hagan; © The Taunton Press, Inc.)

The dead area is removed a little at a time until green, vital wood is revealed. The last cut into green wood is made just above a bud, to let the bud break and allow new growth all the way to the tip. (Photo by Boyd Hagan; © The Taunton Press, Inc.)

The brown shriveled pith of the deadwood on the right is compared to fresh green wood. (Photo by Boyd Hagan; © The Taunton Press, Inc.)

in the spring or, more technically, on the previous season's wood, should not be pruned during the winter. If you prune those shrubs and trees during the winter, you will be cutting off their flower buds, which were formed at the end of the last growing season. Deciduous shrubs and trees that bloom on the previous season's wood should be pruned immediately after they flower during the growing season.

Pruning Schemes

As with timing, different types of plants require different pruning schemes. Informally pruned deciduous shrubs have a different sequence of pruning steps than do deciduous shrubs, subshrubs, deciduous trees, evergreens, evergreen hedges, broad-leaf evergreens, vines, fruiting shrubs and trees, and herbaceous perennials (see Chapter 8, beginning on p. 94). The common guideline for all pruning, though, is sharp, clean, and quick cuts with the right tools.

DECIDUOUS SHRUBS

Deciduous shrubs benefit from several steps of pruning.

Step 1: Remove any dead or dying branches or tips. A dead tip or dying branch will look shriveled, and the bark is often darker than the rest of the branch. Start at the end of the branch and cut a few inches at a time until you see green wood. Make sure that the last cut into green wood is made just below a bud, so the bud will break, causing new growth all the way to the tip.

Step 2: Remove any crossing branches or branches that are growing back toward the main stem(s) of the shrub. This will open up the plant and let in more sunshine as well as focus all branches' growth toward the outside of the plant.

Step 3: Examine the base of the plant and count how many old stems you see as opposed to new suckering growth. Suckers are the young, straight shoots emanating directly from the ground. To completely revitalize the plant, leave all the suckers and cut out all the old stems. This may alter the shape of your landscaping as a whole. If this is too drastic, remove a third of the old stems and continue this practice each year until you have all new growth. By remove, I mean to the ground—no stumps. If you leave stumps, growth will take place off the stumps, and it will not be new, vital growth off the roots of the plant, where flowering will be best.

SUBSHRUBS
Some deciduous shrubs should be cut right to the ground each year before new growth ensues. These plants send up a tremendous amount of growth in one season and bloom only on the new growth. If you leave the old growth, it looks shabby and crowded. These plants are often called subshrubs because they act like herbaceous perennials that die back each year, but the stems of the plants get

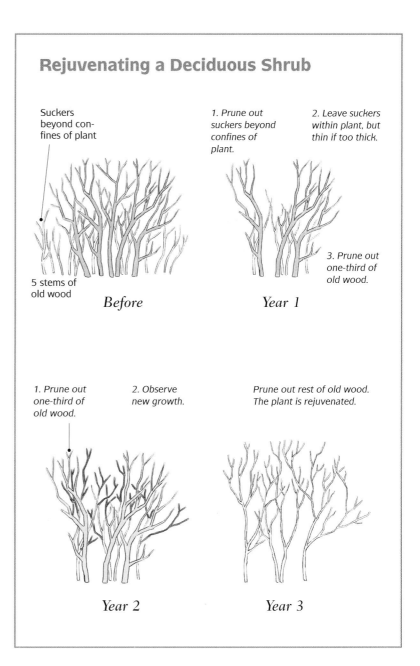

Rejuvenating a Deciduous Shrub

Suckers beyond con-fines of plant

5 stems of old wood

Before

1. Prune out suckers beyond confines of plant.

2. Leave suckers within plant, but thin if too thick.

3. Prune out one-third of old wood.

Year 1

1. Prune out one-third of old wood.

2. Observe new growth.

Year 2

Prune out rest of old wood. The plant is rejuvenated.

Year 3

woody. A few examples are butterfly bush (*Buddleia*), Caryopteris, rose of Sharon (*Hibiscus syriacus*), and Saint-John's-wort (*Hypericum*).

DECIDUOUS HEDGES
Hedges, both deciduous and evergreen, should be pruned with the bottom wider than the top so sunlight can reach the lower half. If the hedge has died out near the bottom, it was probably improperly pruned, and you will have to start over, cutting the

Making a Clean Cut

When you prune to control growth or to remove a few wayward branches on an informally shaped plant, you should always prune each branch individually, making an angled cut, and cleanly cutting just below a bud. Prune the branches arbitrarily so that you are not creating a shape. Minimal pruning can also be achieved by pruning off spent flowers. This paves the way for new growth and next year's flowers.

Cut is made just beyond bud and at an angle.

Correct

Cut is made too close to bud. Bud will dry out.

Incorrect

Cut is made too far from bud. Dead stub will remain.

Incorrect

A subshrub, such as this rose of Sharon, grows from the ground each year after heavy pruning in the fall when frost has killed the topgrowth. Its stems are partially woody, but mostly herbaceous. (Photo by Maureen Gilmer.)

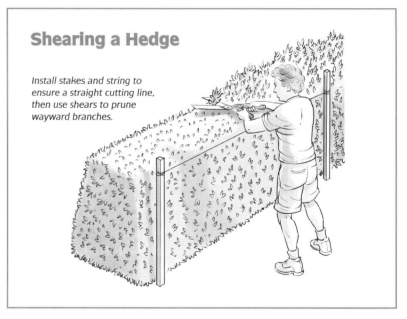

Shearing a Hedge

Install stakes and string to ensure a straight cutting line, then use shears to prune wayward branches.

hedge to within a foot of the ground. You can improve an old, overgrown deciduous hedge in the same way as individual plants: by removing old stems every few years. This will thin the hedge over time. You can also prune the entire hedge to within a foot of the ground, thin out old stems, and let it grow into a new, vital hedge, which it will do within a few years.

If the hedge is too tall or wide, but has leaves to the bottom, you should shear it early in the spring to within 6 in. of where you want it to be. To shear a hedge, install stakes and string to make a straight cutting line at the height you are shearing down to. Use sharp hedge shears and, as you prune branches, be sure the bottom of the hedge is wider than the top to allow sunlight to penetrate to all parts of the plant.

Pruning Roses

There are a few extra precautions you should take when pruning roses. For pruning purposes, roses are distinguished from one another by their blooming schedules and are identified as one of the following: everbloomers, rebloomers, shrubby types, once-bloomers and climbers, species roses, or ramblers. The basic pruning steps for all types of roses follow.

1. Remove any winterkilled stems and branches, cutting back a few inches at a time until you see white pith, the sign of "green" wood in roses.

2. Remove the oldest canes (stems) each year to encourage new cane growth.

3. Prune out any suckers growing from beneath the graft union (knobby area where the topgrowth and the rootstock are joined together), being careful not to damage the graft.

Prune everbloomers and rebloomers when roses are dormant, or first thing in the spring, and again after flowering to remove spent flowers—unless you want the plant to form hips, which are the fruit. When you prune canes, shorten them to three to four buds to promote new growth at the bases of the plants. After pruning, seal all the cuts with nail polish or white glue to keep cane borers from invading the pithy canes.

Some roses flower again in the autumn and need the old flowers removed to encourage this remontant (reblooming) nature. For these roses, you should prune back the flowering stems immediately after blooming to the second five-leaflet node (where the leaflet is attached on the stem), cutting about ¼ in. above the node. In about four to six weeks, the roses will flower again.

Shrub roses should be treated like deciduous shrubs blooming on current season's wood and should be pruned when they're dormant. Remove old canes and reduce the remaining canes to one-half their length. **Once-blooming old roses**, **once-blooming climbers**, **species roses**, and **ramblers** should all be pruned immediately after blooming instead of when they're dormant. Always remove dead, dying, or diseased wood when you see it, at any time of year.

Pruning Everblooming and Reblooming Roses

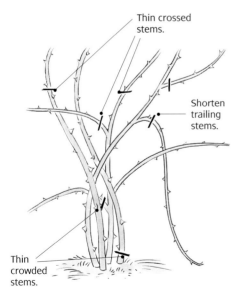

Thin crossed stems.

Shorten trailing stems.

Thin crowded stems.

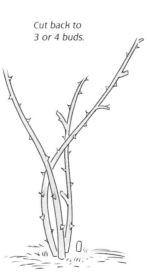

Cut back to 3 or 4 buds.

Cutting Back Spent Flowers on Reblooming Roses

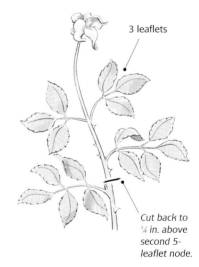

3 leaflets

Cut back to ¼ in. above second 5-leaflet node.

Don't Top Your Trees

When shaping a deciduous tree, do not "top" it by cutting off the leader stem. This is a favorite pastime of electric company linesmen who remove branches from under electric lines. When you cut off the main leader of a tree, it will not grow again. Even if a new branch becomes dominant and tries to take over, it will form a U shape from the cut leader and bend out before growing straight again, mis-shaping the tree. The rest of the branches will continue their upward growth around the missing center, which also looks strange.

Sometimes an insect will bore into the leader and kill it, which is particularly noticeable in softwoods like pine. If the leader stem is pruned off or destroyed by disease or insects, the tree will always look like a wide, bushy shrub instead of a tree because it grows out and not up. So, unless you are purposely pollarding (a pruning technique that stubs back all growth) for ornamental purposes, avoid the practice of cutting back the leader. If height is a problem, you are better off buying a smaller species of tree to fit the situation.

Topping trees distorts the natural shape of the tree by cutting off the main leader, which will never grow back again in the same way. (Photo by Richard Shiell.)

DECIDUOUS TREES

An overgrown tree can be revitalized, but it is sometimes a tricky and dangerous job better left to the professional arborist. Large trees can be thinned in the crown, but this work must be done from the cage of a cherry-picker or by an expert climbing arborist who uses ropes to brace himself and the branches he is cutting off. Dwarf ornamental trees, on the other hand, can be easily tackled by the homeowner. Some of the same principles of pruning deciduous shrubs are used.

Step 1: Remove dead and dying branches. Then remove crossing branches and those headed back into the trunk. If there are branches headed straight to the ground, remove those as well.

Step 2: Remove any suckers emanating from the main trunk at ground level. These are usually suckering off of the rootstock, not the upper part of the plant.

Step 3: Examine the shape of the crown or head of the tree. It is best to confine your pruning to small branches (less than 1½ in. in diameter), so as not to change the

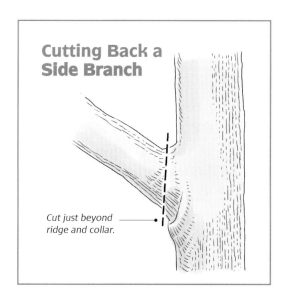

Cutting Back a Side Branch

Cut just beyond ridge and collar.

Plants that grow with layered branches are easily pruned, creating a natural covering to the pruning cut. Once the dead portion is removed, the next layer of green leaves falls over the cut, making it invisible.
(Photos by Judi Rutz; © The Taunton Press, Inc.)

whole outline of the tree. You can head a tree up higher so it can be walked under by removing the lowest branches (one or two per year as it grows taller), but be careful not to "flush cut" the branches back to the trunk. I am not suggesting you leave a large stub, but a flush cut will damage the collar (point of attachment to the trunk) of the branch. The collar is usually somewhat raised and obvious. Cut just beyond the collar, and the wound will overgrow and prevent disease from entering it or sprouts growing from it.

HEALTHY PRUNING

Resist the urge to cover pruning cuts with any kind of Band-Aid. Covering a pruning cut with tar or other substance is no longer considered a healthy practice. Instead of helping the wound to heal, it holds in moisture, creating just the right environment for insects and diseases to proliferate.

Step 4: If you have to cut a large branch, it is important to do it in stages so the bark will not rip or peel below the wound. Remove some of the weight of the branch a few feet at a time until you are within a foot of the trunk or limb. Make your next cut under the branch about a third of the way through on the branch side of the collar. Your final cut will be on the top of the branch to meet the undercut.

EVERGREENS

If evergreen shrubs and trees are overgrown, it is usually because they are too big for the situation they are in. They rarely need pruning for maintenance as they mature. It is best to move the tree or shrub if it is small enough to move, or remove it completely and start over with an evergreen better suited to the site.

Shrubby evergreens can be pruned by removing a wayward branch just below another layer of growth that is at an acceptable length and will cover the pruned branch. Junipers are easily kept in check this way because they usually grow in layers.

You can slow down the growth of evergreens and make them more bushy by pinching back the new growth of whorled evergreens. (Photo by Susan Kahn; © The Taunton Press, Inc.)

Break off the candles of pines to slow their growth. (Photo by Susan Kahn; © The Taunton Press, Inc.)

Leggy rhododendron can be encouraged to bush out by pinching off the vegetative buds. Be sure to choose the smaller terminal buds rather than the fatter flower buds or you will remove the flowers.
(Photo by Lee Reich; © The Taunton Press, Inc.)

Of course, dead and dying branches should be pruned off, and hedges should be pruned to allow sunlight to reach the lower levels. (As with deciduous hedges, the bottom half should be wider than the top half.) If they have not been properly pruned and the bottoms are dead, you will be hard-pressed to rejuvenate the hedge. To lower a hedge, you should reach within it and select branches to prune out either at their source or low enough that the cut will be covered by another branch. It is best to renovate over several years because many evergreens do not respond favorably to severe pruning.

You can slow down regrowth of evergreens by pinching back or breaking off the candles (the soft new growth from the center of the whorl of branches) with your fingers. This either partially or completely removes the new growth, depending on whether you remove part or all of the candle. The result will contain the plant, but it will be a never-ending annual battle. You are better off buying a plant that grows to the right size to begin with. If a plant is thin because it was growing too close to another plant that has since been removed or was shaded by a plant that has been removed, you can attempt to make it denser by partially pinching back the candles. It will take a few years to see results.

In general, broadleaf evergreens, such as rhododendrons, do not respond well to major renovation. Leggy rhododendron plants can be pinched back where the new growth appears after flowering to encourage bushing out. You also can try cutting back to within a foot or so of the ground, but it will take a long time, if ever, for the plant to recover.

Don't shear the top of the plant; instead, cut individual stems back to branches lower on the plant. It's best to do a few stems every year rather than a wholesale pruning in one year. There is more chance for the plant to recover if the renovation is done this way.

VINES

You can fully renovate most vines, such as honeysuckle (*Lonicera sempervirens*), English ivy (*Hedera helix*), and silver lace vine (*Polygonum aubertii*), by cutting to the ground and waiting for new sprouts to appear. Then treat the vine as if it were new, and train the young stems on a trellis or other structure. If this is too drastic, prune as for deciduous shrubs: early bloomers after they flower, summer bloomers while they are dormant. Old stems should be removed completely along with dead and dying plant parts. A few stems pruned in this way each year will keep a vine vital and flowering and will prevent it from becoming an overgrown mess.

SMALL FRUITS

Whether in bush or vine form, the easiest way to prune small fruits, such as raspberries, is by cutting them to the ground while they are dormant. You will lose a year of fruit but, presumably, they were not bearing well anyway if they were neglected.

Alternatively, you can prune as with other deciduous shrubs and remove a third of the old canes each year until you have a new plant in year four. When you remove the old canes, you will also want to shorten the remaining canes because they will tumble over without the support of their old friends. Observe where the remains of old fruit first show on the lower part of the stems and cut to that point.

FRUIT TREES

Some old fruit trees just aren't worth keeping. An old, neglected fruit tree is usually an eyesore, and it probably isn't very productive or is of a variety not worth producing. There have been many improvements in fruit trees over the years, and an old standard-sized apple tree that has been bored into by insects and disease is not a keeper. Chances

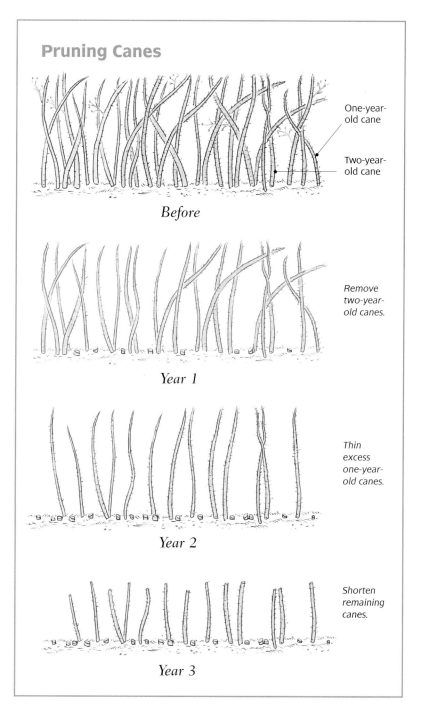

Pruning Canes

One-year-old cane

Two-year-old cane

Before

Remove two-year-old canes.

Year 1

Thin excess one-year-old canes.

Year 2

Shorten remaining canes.

Year 3

are the tree is too large and ungainly, too. Some fruit trees, like peaches, are short-lived anyway.

The best solution is to take down the tree and plant improved dwarf and semi-dwarf fruit trees, which are easier to take care of, prune, and harvest from. Dwarf doesn't mean less fruit; dwarf apple trees, for instance, get to be 10 ft. to 15 ft. tall with enough fruit to supply you and several of your neighbors.

If you inherited an orchard and are interested in production, aesthetics may not be a concern, but getting the trees back into production will be a chore. It requires several steps and several years to bring the trees back to full bearing status. All the branches must be opened up to the light to produce flowers and fruit. This requires pruning of major limbs as well as smaller ones.

You should not remove more than one or two major limbs in a growing season, and, for that reason, it may take a few years to complete the pruning job. Remember, these trees have been shaded for many years by overgrowth. Opening them up too fast will subject them to the burning rays of the sun, which, during the winter, will cause the bark to crack and split. An already weak fruit tree may not survive that torture.

Pruning an Old Fruit Tree

Thin out crossing, dead, or dying branches.

Remove one or two old limbs back to the trunk to open up the tree to the light. This may need to be done over a few seasons to acclimate the bark to the new light.

COMPANIONS FOR TREES

If you like the shape of your old apple tree, and it is not about to fall down, you can dress it up for ornamental purposes by planting climbing vines in it and using it as a support for the vines. Prune out rotten (soft, weak) branches, but leave dry, dead limbs. Prune out any suckering branches and just leave the main structure of the tree. Plant climbing roses at its base and they will clamber up the tree.

Step 1: Carefully examine all parts of the tree to be sure you are not choosing to keep weak branches with hollows caused by boring insects and pecking birds (who were going after the insects). Remove all dead, dying, or diseased wood and then remove one or two major branches all the way back to the trunk unless there are side branches strong enough to take over. In that case, cut back to the side branch on the major limb. You can consider aesthetics if you want, but if the tree was pruned in the past for production, it is probably not a pretty sight. It will be hard to make it pretty and productive, especially if it was neglected.

Step 2: Examine the remaining branches of the tree. Prune out crossing branches and those that have weak crotches. (A crotch is where two branches emerge together in a V shape.) Unless both branches of the crotch are sturdy and not impeding each other or other branches, select the best situated of the two and prune out the other. Any branch that droops toward the ground (unless the tree has a naturally weeping habit) or points back in toward the trunk should also be removed.

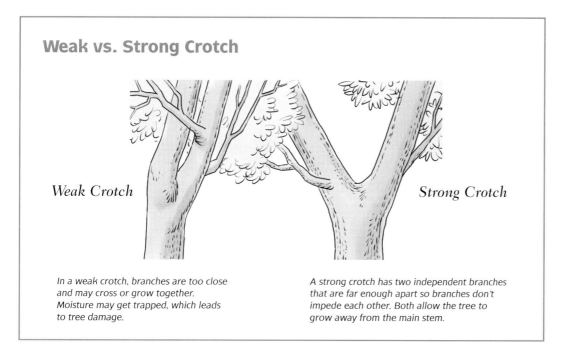
Step 3: Once you have removed old branches, new branches will sprout from the cuts. Sometimes, they will look like a witches' broom. This happens to many deciduous plants, and fruit trees in particular. Select the best and strongest branch at each cut and remove the others. These cuts may continue to generate new growth. You will have to pay attention to all subsequent cuts that you make over the years and repeat this selection process.

Many old apple trees actually have holes in the main trunk, usually where branches have pruned themselves off because of weight. Sometimes these holes were made by insects and have been enlarged by bur-rowing animals or nesting birds. Usually, the tree has healed itself by overgrowing the edges, and although the hole remains, it is of no consequence to the tree unless it has made it so weak that it is ready to break off at the wound. Use a sharp pruning knife to remove any craggy bark edges. If the hole fills with water, it is OK—leave it alone at this point. The temptation is to fill the hole with some compound, but it is not necessary and may even cause more harm than good by creating a moist haven for insects and disease.

Next Steps

Even with the pruning job complete, you have only just begun to rejuvenate a planting. The next step is to improve the quality of your soil with amendments like fertilizer, lime, and compost. Then you must mulch to conserve moisture, and water properly and adequately. The time that you take now to begin the rejuvenation process will pay off later with a landscape that is pleasing and enjoyable.

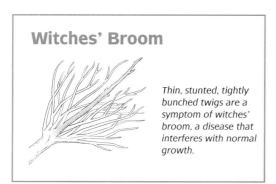

The hole in this tree was made by a falling limb. It has healed itself and requires no further help. Do not fill the hole because it will create a moist haven for insects and disease. (Photo by Judi Rutz; © The Taunton Press, Inc.)

8 Timely Transplanting

Transplanting is the method used to remove a plant from one place and put it in another. Those plants you have decided to keep but would like to move to another part of the yard qualify for this treatment. All plants—trees and shrubs, evergreen and deciduous, perennials and bulbs— can be transplanted. The most important considerations for successful transplanting are timing, tools, and technique. Trees and shrubs have similar requirements in those areas, but perennials and bulbs are treated very differently.

A crowded planting bed like this would benefit by transplanting and division of perennials. Also, some lower-growing perennials have become obscured by taller ones in front of them, and the house windows are threatened by giant plants best grown in another part of the yard.
(Photo by Delilah Smittle; © The Taunton Press. Inc.)

fessional with a mechanical tree spade, it will be expensive, and it is risky because you are cutting off over half of the tree's root system. In many cases, it is smarter to just cut the tree down and put a younger tree in the new spot.

Timing Is Everything

When you plant trees and shrubs purchased at a garden center, either containerized or balled and burlapped (B & B), you are transplanting them from the nursery in which they were grown. The difference between those plants and the ones growing in your yard is that yours have spread their roots and have grown undisturbed until now. On the other hand, a B & B plant has been in a holding pattern since it was dug in the nursery, and it has recovered from the shock of digging even though much of its root system was cut off. It is ready at any time of the growing season to be put back into the ground and to start growing again.

A plant that was grown from its inception in a container, either from seed or cutting, will suffer only a slight disturbance when removed from the container, therefore it also can be transplanted at any time of the growing season. However, the plants in the ground in your yard can only be transplanted at certain times of the year, or they will not survive having their roots disturbed.

In general, there are better times of the year to transplant than others, although, with precautions mentioned below, it is possible to transplant during risky times, such as the middle of the summer when it is hot and dry. The least risky time for deciduous plants is before the buds begin to swell or leaves appear in spring, *or* after they have dropped their leaves in fall and gone into dormancy. There is a larger window for evergreens, which can be transplanted after the new growth candles (see p. 90 for a

Size Spells Success

The size of a tree or shrub at the time it is transplanted will have a direct impact on recovery time and success. The smaller the tree or shrub, the quicker it will recover from transplanting, and the more likely it will thrive. If you have a big tree (larger than 6 in. in caliper, which is the diameter of the stem or trunk 6 in. above the ground) and you want to move it, think twice about the effort and the expense. You will need a pro-

Measuring a Root Ball to Plant at the Correct Depth

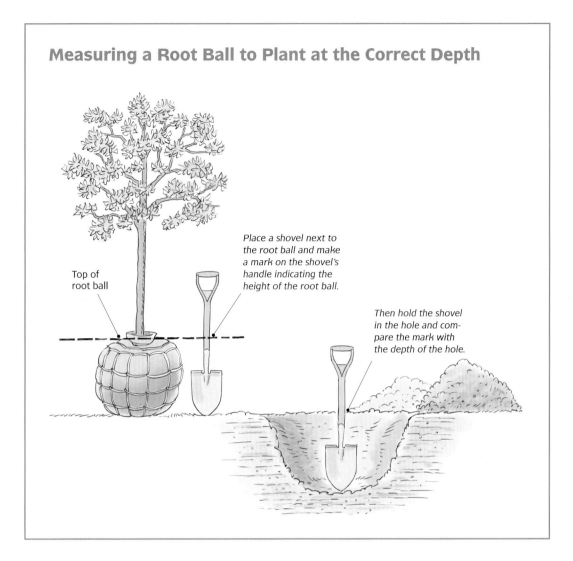

Top of root ball

Place a shovel next to the root ball and make a mark on the shovel's handle indicating the height of the root ball.

Then hold the shovel in the hole and compare the mark with the depth of the hole.

description of the candles) have hardened off (become stiff, no longer soft and supple) in late spring, and throughout the summer into dormancy in fall. Broadleaf evergreens, such as rhododendrons, should be transplanted at the same time as deciduous plants.

Time your transplanting so that you can replant as soon as possible after you dig up the plant. Have the new hole at least partially predug. You should leave it just shy of the final depth until you determine the exact size of the root ball on the plant you are moving. You can't judge the size of the root ball until the plant is completely out of the ground.

Measure the root ball by holding your shovel or spade next to it and marking its height on the handle. Hold the shovel in the hole and compare the mark you've made with the hole depth. You do not want to replant any deeper than the plant was before. In fact, it is better if the hole is a little shallow than too deep.

TRENCHING
Sometimes plants must be moved before their new space is ready for them. If the plants need to be held for a few days, they can be moved to the shade in a site accessible to water and the root balls can be mulched in with shredded bark mulch. If they need to be held for a few weeks or

Trees Held Over in Trench

For plants that must be held over for a few weeks before planting, dig a trench and cover the root balls with mulch. Be sure to water them regularly.

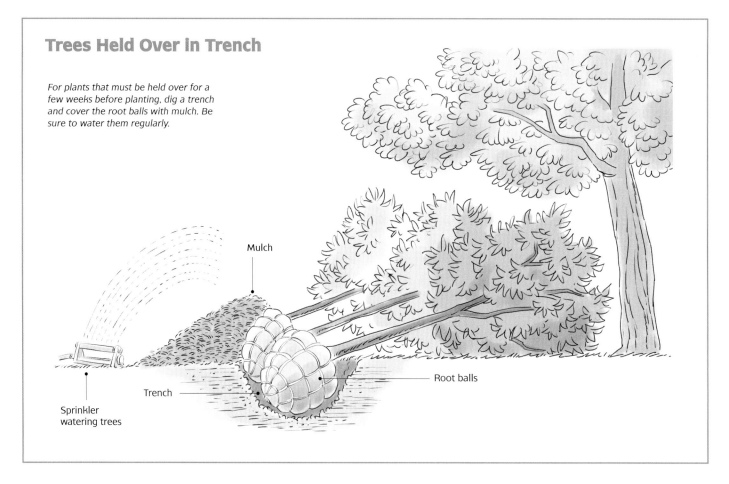

Mulch

Trench

Root balls

Sprinkler watering trees

even months, it is best to dig a trench in a shaded site near water, lay the plants in the trench, and cover the root balls with soil and mulch. Either way, the plants should be checked regularly for moisture, and a sprinkler should be set up to keep them moist, but not soaked.

Test the moisture level with your hand by sticking it deeply into the mulch and soil near the root balls. Be aware that the longer the plants must be held in limbo before permanent planting in the new site, the greater the risk to their survival.

REDUCING THE RISK TO VULNERABLE PLANTS

Occasionally, because of the timing of building construction, a plant must be transplanted when it is most vulnerable, even if it is not advisable because its chances of survival are diminished. To reduce risk, water-soak the plants to be

moved for a few days prior to transplanting, then dig them according to the techniques that follow. All plants need water and lots of it after they are transplanted, but this preliminary soaking will be helpful.

Because plants suffer moisture loss through their leaves, it's a good idea to prune back deciduous plants as much as a foot before transplanting to reduce moisture loss, no matter when you transplant. You also can spray the plant, whether evergreen or deciduous, with an antidessicant, which guards against moisture loss through the leaves (available at your local garden center).

A landscaping trick of the trade is to remove *all* the leaves of a tree or shrub if it is being transplanted at a risky time of year. The branches are left intact, but all leaves are stripped from the tree. If it survives the move, the tree or shrub will grow a new set of leaves, perhaps a little smaller, before the end of the growing season.

Keep in mind that when you transplant at the correct times of the year, you can expect a loss of plants as great as 20 percent. When you choose a risky time of year to transplant, you increase the chance of losses to 50 percent or more, so do what you can to avoid transplanting at bad times.

The Right Tools for the Job

As for most jobs, the proper tools can make the difference between success and failure. This is just as important for transplanting as it is for pruning. Think of transplanting as pruning below ground. Roots should not be squashed or peeled any more than branches above ground should be, nor should they be subjected to disease by using unclean shovels and pruners. Sharp, clean tools allow for a quicker, safer recovery for your plants and make the job easier on you.

You will need hand pruners, loppers, and a saw for stubborn roots, as well as a shovel and spade with sharpened blades. Have biodegradable burlap (never plastic) and twine ready to surround the root ball before it is moved, and have a method for moving the tree once it is dug up. A professional uses a skid-steer loader with a bucket or forks attached to hold the tree or shrub. Nurseries have special "tree handlers," which attach to the front of a machine like a skid-steer loader and have adjustable fork-like protrusions at ground level to hold the root ball and steadying arms 3 ft. to 4 ft. higher to embrace the upper part of the tree as it is being moved.

Landscapers and others who do a lot of transplanting have a tree cart, which is like

Give Your Plants Protection

If you don't want to risk killing your plants by moving them at the wrong time of year, but need to protect them during building construction on your property, you can leave them in place if you take protective measures. Buy some orange mesh construction cloth and stakes, which are manufactured specifically for this purpose, to mark off the areas around the plants. Alternatively, and perhaps even smarter, use snow fencing and stakes. These work well because snow fencing is made of wood and wire, which is more sturdy and may be "felt" more easily by an operator on a machine backing up toward a tree. Make it even more noticeable by spray-painting it with orange blazes.

The placement of either material is crucial. It does no good to put the fencing right next to the plants. You must place it far enough away from the plants to account for their spreading roots underground. Roots should not be driven over by cars, let alone bulldozers and backhoes. Constant foot traffic, piles of gravel, and construction debris over shallow roots can be just as harmful. So look at the crowns of trees and the spread of shrubs and stake off these plants in correlation to the size of their tops.

In addition, speak to the foreman on the job about dumping materials away from roots, and keep a watchful eye on the fencing throughout construction—it is very easy for temporary fencing to fall down or be moved. Remember, no one is going to care more about your plants than you.

(Photo by Boyd Hagan; © The Taunton Press, Inc.)

Tools for transplanting from left to right: hand trowel, spade, small shovel, mattock with pick, rake, fork, large round-headed shovel. (Photo by Boyd Hagan; © The Taunton Press, Inc.)

a tree handler but is on wheels to eliminate the need for a machine. If you have a lot of plants to move, you can rent a skid-steer loader or a tree cart. You'll need two people—one to guide the cart or machine to the new site and another to steady the tree along the way. If the job doesn't justify the rental, you can try using a wheelbarrow, although the height of the wheelbarrow may be too high to lift the tree and root ball up and over.

Moving Trees

Trees are the most difficult plants to move. By virtue of their size alone, it is difficult to dig through their chunky roots, lift them out of the hole, move them to the next site, and replant them. Depending on the size of the tree, you may decide to hire a professional to dig by hand or dig with a mechanical tree spade. However, any tree less than 2 in. in caliper can usually be handled by most homeowners as long as they have the right tools.

A tree cart provides transportation for trees with a minimum of effort. (Photo by Boyd Hagan; © The Taunton Press, Inc.)

Trees on the Move

Here are two tried-and-true low-tech methods for moving trees. For either one, you'll need to recruit helpers with a strong back and arms.

Sling Method

A burlap sling provides a handhold for two people as another steadies the tree.

Roller System

This roller system, built from plywood and 4-in. PVC pipe, is helpful when moving heavy objects, like large trees.

Step 1: Tie up all evergreen branches and wide-spreading deciduous tree branches before breaking ground so the branches will be out of the way and there will be no danger of breaking them during the move (see photo A). To tie up branches, simply wrap baling twine around the branches and tug on the twine to pull them closer to the main trunk. Healthy, vital tree branches will not snap off with this treatment.

Step 2: Gather your transplanting tools. In order to determine how large to make the root ball, look at the crown of the tree. The root ball should be the same diameter as the crown for trees with less than 2½ in. caliper. Trees of this size usually have crowns about 2 ft. to 2½ ft. across. This is how wide you'll need to make the circle of cuts. Of course, the larger the tree, the lar-

Lace up an evergreen or deciduous tree or shrub to avoid branch breakage during moving and transplanting. (Photos by Boyd Hagan; © The Taunton Press, Inc.)

Start digging some distance from the shrub or tree you are transplanting by using a sharp spade, which is straight edged and flat. It will cut with the right camber straight through roots. (Photo by Boyd Hagan; © The Taunton Press, Inc.)

B

Correlation between Tree Crown and Root Ball

Head of tree is equal to diameter of root ball on trees with less than 2½-in. caliper.

er the root ball, but the root balls of very large trees are condensed a bit and not as large as the crown.

Step 3: Use a handheld spade to make the first cuts into the ground around the tree (see photo B). (A spade is the perfect tool for this job—it is the correct shape and length and has the right camber for these first cuts.) Push straight down into the ground with the spade and your foot. If the blade is sharp enough, it will cut right through roots as it enters. Cut a circle completely around the tree with the spade.

Step 4: With a round-headed shovel, continue to dig the root ball from the outside edge of the circle (see photo C). You can always pare down the size of the root ball a bit if you find no roots to the outside of the ball, but you can never go bigger, so give the ball ample size during this first digging.

Continue around the circumference of the ball to a depth of at least 2 ft. to 2½ ft.

for a 2-in. caliper tree. You can reduce that depth incrementally a few inches for smaller trees. For example, a 1½-in. caliper tree should have a root ball 1½ ft. to 2 ft. in depth. Reach the spade straight under the ball to cut any roots under it. You might need a helper to rock and hold the tree forward in order to get under it.

Step 5: If you come up against a very large root or one that gives you trouble because it is situated under the ball you are making, you will need another cutting tool to get the

Use a round-headed shovel to continue digging after the initial cuts with the spade. Continue to dig from the outside edge, giving the root ball ample width and depth. (Photo by Boyd Hagan; © The Taunton Press, Inc.)

job done. Use pruners, loppers, a pruning saw, or sharp spade blade to cut those roots cleanly just as you would a branch above ground (see photo D). Do not twist, shred, or peel roots because damaged roots cannot draw in water and nutrients from the soil.

Step 6: Before you lift the tree and root ball out of the ground, wet down a piece of burlap and lay it beside the hole. Set the tree down on the burlap and wrap the burlap around the root ball (see photo E on p. 105). Do this even if you are moving the tree immediately into its new hole. It is critical to keep disturbance of the roots to a minimum, including having soil drop from the roots and exposing them to the atmosphere. If you are moving the tree to a temporary trench, tie baling twine around the

Stubborn roots can be sliced cleanly with hand pruners, loppers (for bigger roots), or even a pruning saw (for large roots). (Photo by Boyd Hagan; © The Taunton Press, Inc.)

THE BEST TWINE FOR TYING

Baling twine is the best twine to use for tying up tree branches. It's the same twine that's used on farms to hold together bales of hay. It is strong and reliable, but it won't cut through bark or roots. Unlike plastic twine, it is biodegradable. Baling twine is always used in nurseries for tying up plants and root balls. You can find it at farm-supply stores in large rolls.

Staking Trees

Trees are staked for a purpose, not for show. Until their roots can reestablish, they need help to combat gusty winds. Unfortunately, many staking jobs are poorly done, and the stakes do little more than window dress. Trees that are staked improperly end up growing sideways into maturity.

Evergreens are staked with three short stakes placed at equal intervals around the tree with as much stake buried in the ground as is seen above ground. The stakes are usually 3 ft. to 4 ft. long and made of hardwood or softwood 2-in. by 2-in. stock. It doesn't matter that the stakes will rot. By the time they do, they will not be needed anymore. The stakes are pounded in at an angle away from the tree, about 18 in. away from the circumference of the branches.

The best way to attach the stakes to the tree is with electric fence wire. First, protect the tree from the wire with a length of old rubber or plastic hose about 14 in. long. (You'll need one piece of hose for each stake.) Slip the wire through the hose and wrap the hose around the trunk of the tree, at waist height. Pull the hose as a loop toward the stake. Secure the wire by twisting together at the stake. Pull the wire taut by slipping one handle of a set of pruners through the two wires and twisting them around each other. Do this for all three stakes. Remember, the wire must be taut for the stakes to do any good.

Deciduous trees are staked with two long stakes at least 6 ft. long, with 2 ft. buried in the ground, evenly spaced and opposite each other about 2 ft. from the tree. The stakes should be straight, all at the same height above ground, and oriented to let the prevailing wind slip by. The wiring procedure is identical to that of evergreens, but the wire is pulled taut absolutely parallel to the ground.

Stakes on any kind of tree should be checked regularly to make sure the wires are still taut. They usually can be removed about a year after planting, unless the trees are planted in a particularly windy location and need more time to get established. When it's time, just remove the wires and hose, and break the stakes off at ground level.

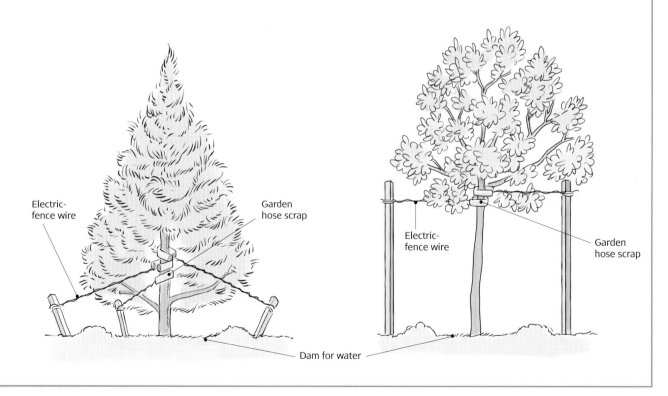

Electric-fence wire

Garden hose scrap

Dam for water

Electric-fence wire

Garden hose scrap

burlap to hold it in place. Leave the branches tied up unless the tree will be there for more than a few days. In that case, untie the branches to give them breathing room.

Step 7: Before replanting, measure the root ball and compare its depth to the new hole. Adjust the depth accordingly, cut open the branches of the tree, and set the tree into the hole with its best side facing in the right direction. You can turn it slightly in the hole, but every movement rubs roots and disturbs the ball, so try to pick the best side before putting it in the hole.

Make sure the tree is straight (it is easiest to have one person hold it straight while another backfills), cut any strings on the burlap, and peel back the burlap and roll it down to the bottom of the hole. Do not attempt to remove the burlap unless you can do so without disturbing the ball at all. The burlap will biodegrade in place.

If you are going to add soil amendments, such as fertilizer, do so before you put the tree in the hole. Work the fertilizer into the soil in the hole and into the soil you will use to backfill the hole.

Step 8: Backfill the hole with the soil you removed. Fill in about a foot and stomp with your heel around the root ball to pack the soil in and remove air pockets, much like packing brown sugar in a measuring cup. Repeat the filling and packing until you have reached the top, being sure to quit at the original soil line of the root ball. Make a dam around the tree to a distance equivalent to the root ball diameter and fill it with water.

Step 9: Continue watering for the next three days with a drip-type irrigation system or a very slow hose. It is better for the tree to receive a little water for a long time than a lot of water for a short time. Mulch with

E

Wrap the root ball with burlap, even if you are transplanting immediately, to minimize disturbance and loss of soil. (Photo by Boyd Hagan; © The Taunton Press, Inc.)

shredded bark to a depth of 3 in. around the base of the tree, out as far as the dam. This will hold in moisture and keep weeds and lawnmowers away from the base of the tree.

Step 10: Stake the tree according to the directions in "Staking Trees."

Moving Shrubs

Evergreen and deciduous shrubs are transplanted in the same way evergreen and deciduous trees are transplanted. The only difference is that the size of the root ball is smaller unless the shrub is as big as a 2-in. caliper tree.

You can gauge the size of the root ball by the width of the overall shrub stems. The root ball is about two-thirds the diameter of the shrubbery. Add 6 in. to the diameter when you make your first cuts into the ground. Again, you can always shave off excess if need be, but you can't add back to roots once they are cut, so be generous with the root ball. The fewer roots cut off, the more quickly and easily the shrub will acclimate to its new space.

Dividing and Moving Perennials

Perennials are not pruned as shrubs and trees are, instead they are divided. With age, most perennials like daylilies (*Hemerocallis* spp.), hosta, and black-eyed Susan form

Masses of black-eyed Susans beg for division. Division revitalizes and reshapes old plants. (Photo courtesy *Fine Gardening* magazine; © The Taunton Press, Inc.)

Shrub Root Ball Size

Root ball should be two-thirds the diameter of top of shrub.

large masses in the garden. To revitalize old plants and reshape them, they are divided. And in the course of dividing plants, you must transplant them. Of course, if you need to move a whole clump of perennials you can, but they will benefit by division at the same time. The bonus by-products of division are the resulting "new" plants divided off the old clumps, which you can then transplant to another part of the garden.

Division can be done at any time of the growing season, but the best time is before the plants start to regrow in the spring. This is because the foliage will not be spoiled by chopping, moving, and moisture loss, and the plants will have time to reestablish themselves during the growing season. Usually, plant roots will not be harmed by a middle-of-the-season move as long as they are not allowed to dry out. Foliage will droop, though, and should be cut back by half to reduce moisture loss. It will grow back during the season.

You may want to wait until after a plant has flowered to divide or transplant it, so you can enjoy the flowers for that season, but culturally, it doesn't really matter with most perennials when they are divided or transplanted. A few, such as peonies, are pickier and slow to reestablish, so it is worth the effort of looking up culture instructions in a plant encyclopedia to determine which plants should be left alone or should be composted if they must be removed from an area and resent transplanting.

The best tools to use for dividing are a sharp spade and garden fork, although a round- or flat-headed shovel will do. Again, you want to make clean cuts to the roots, so the sharper the spade blade, the better.

Start with a large tined garden fork and wiggle it down into the clump of foliage at the point you wish to divide. Sometimes, especially if the soil is loose and malleable,

you can pull apart and separate a clump away from the main clump with just the fork. It is also helpful to use two forks, back-to-back, to tease apart the divisions.

For fleshy and woody-centered perennials, such as hosta, you will need to make a clean cut with a spade or shovel straight down through the foliage and roots to completely divide the plant. Make sure you include several developing buds in each division. Then dig 3 in. to 4 in. away from the outside circumference of the plant as you would a shrub, with enough depth to get most of the roots. As with shrubs and trees, overkill is better, and you can always shake away excess soil or shave the root ball. Wrap with wet burlap and move to the new hole or mulch in a trench in cool shade if you must hold the plants for a while. Replant as you would a tree or shrub.

Dividing with Forks Back-to-Back

Use two large garden forks to separate and divide perennials.

Above and right: When dividing and moving perennials, make a clean cut straight down through the middle of the plant, including several developing buds in each division. (Photos by Sloan Howard; © The Taunton Press, Inc.)

Moving Bulbs

Bulbous plants—those with bulbs, tubers (swollen roots used for food storage), or rhizomes (swollen, underground stems), such as tulips, daffodils, dahlias, and iris—differ from perennials in the timing of division or transplanting and in their storage. Under normal circumstances, spring-flowering bulbs such as tulips and daffodils are left in the ground over the winter.

Summer-flowering bulbs, such as dahlias and gladiolas, must always be lifted and stored for the winter in anticipation of replanting in the spring.

For the most part, spring-flowering bulbs are left alone unless they are mature and their flowering has diminished over the years. If flowering is sparse, this is usually because they are overcrowded. Divide these bulbs before they start to grow in the spring or after they are dormant in the fall (after the deciduous trees have lost their leaves). Division allows the bulbs to grow during the growing season and to store food and energy for the next bloom.

Use a garden fork to dig under the bulbs and lift them out of the ground as a clump. Shake off the soil, and separate them into individual bulbs. Replant them at three to

Use a garden fork to dig under the bulbs and lift them to the surface as a clump. Shake off soil, and separate them into individual bulbs. (Photo by Boyd Hagan; © The Taunton Press, Inc.)

Overcrowded bulbs benefit by lifting and division. Divide daffodils and tulips before they start to grow in spring or after they are dormant in the fall. (Photo by Steve Silk; © The Taunton Press, Inc.)

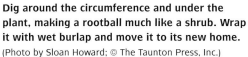

Dig around the circumference and under the plant, making a rootball much like a shrub. Wrap it with wet burlap and move it to its new home. (Photo by Sloan Howard; © The Taunton Press, Inc.)

five times their own depth and two to three bulb widths apart.

If bulbs need to be moved to another area but don't need dividing, you can lift them with a shovel, spade, or fork, soil and all, in full growth right after they flower or as the leaves start to die down after flowering. Replant them *immediately* in their new spot. They will continue to die down naturally.

If bulbs need to be held for a period of time, lift them when the leaves begin to yellow after flowering, clean them of soil, and lay them out to dry overnight on a wire-mesh tray. Then dust them with fungicide and store them in paper bags (never plastic) in a dry, frost-free area until the next planting season (for tulips and daffodils this is the fall). Lift summer-flowering bulbs after the foliage is blackened by the first frost and treat them in the same way.

9 Renovating the Front Entry: Stoops and Steps

There is no more important and exposed area in your yard than the front entry. For many people, the front entry is what landscaping is all about. This is the first space your guests see and the area people look at when they drive by. The front entry is not lived in like the backyard and patio are (unless you have a glorious front porch), but it probably receives more traffic than those spaces ever will. Also, the front entry is the primary outside area most people fix up when they want to sell their homes because this is where potential buyers receive their first impressions.

The front entry is the first place your guests see and the area people look at when they drive by. It creates a first impression about all of your property. (Photo courtesy *Fine Homebuilding* magazine; © The Taunton Press, Inc.)

The front entry includes the front door, stoop, steps, walkway, and plantings. (Photo by Charles Miller; © The Taunton Press, Inc.)

The front entry is comprised of the front door, stoop, steps, walkway, and plantings. Often, there is more than one entry at the front of the house—it may be a door to the kitchen or mudroom. Both entries may have the same components, but they should be treated differently to place emphasis on the door you want your guests to use. The main entry is usually larger in scale with a stoop and steps able to accommodate two people side by side. It should be inviting and safe, properly lit, and easily negotiable. In this chapter, I will discuss the first areas of the entry you must address, the stoop and steps. The walkway must also be taken into consideration when you renovate these areas, but it has its own set of conditions and will be discussed in the next chapter.

Start with an Assessment

The best way to attack the stoop and steps is to assess their problems. First, you will need to figure out what material they are constructed from and, in the case of concrete, whether or not they are attached integrally to the foundation of your house. The three most common reasons for renovation are size, shape, and poor state of repair, so during your assessment, no matter what the material, ask yourself these questions:

• Is the size of the stoop and step system in scale with the front facade of the house? Is it adequate for at least two people to stand on side by side without moving off of it for an opening door?

• Is the shape appropriate and interesting?

• What state of repair is it in?

Most front stoops are prefabricated out of concrete and set in place in front of the threshold of the door. A few steps are usually built into the stoop, and the whole system can be as narrow as the door itself or much wider, stretching across part of the front of the house.

These detached concrete systems are prone to several problems, especially after they've been in place for a number of years. Settling is the worst problem, and it causes the riser or step up to the door threshold to be larger than it should be and not equal with the risers of the built-in steps. Settling can also cause the whole system to be cockeyed against the foundation. The surface of the concrete can become discolored and pitted with age, and hairline cracks can develop from years of freeze/thaw cycles

or use of deicer. If your house has no gutters or porch covering the front stoop, there may be an indentation, directly under the roof line, which has been carved by ice and rain. Another problem is size. The stoop may be out of scale with the doorway, the walkway, or even the house if you have made additions to your house over the years. Finally, some people think concrete is just plain ugly.

Occasionally, the concrete stoop and steps are poured together with the founda-

Detached concrete stoops and steps placed next to the foundation can settle and become discolored and pitted with age. (Photo by Boyd Hagan; © The Taunton Press, Inc.)

Attached concrete stoops and steps are poured with the foundation, often to create a footing for a masonary finish. They cannot be separated without spoiling the integrity of the front foundation, but they can be repaired. (Photo by Boyd Hagan; © The Taunton Press, Inc.)

tion and cannot be separated without spoiling the integrity of the front foundation. The all-in-one stoop, steps, and foundation is often constructed that way to provide a footing for a masonry finish like bricks or flagstone. If the budget ran out, it may never have been covered with the paving stone. If the concrete was covered, there may be cracks in the paving stones or grout, which make the stoop and steps unsightly. It also may be out of scale or too small for the space, or you may want it to be another shape.

Another common building material for stoops and steps is wood. As with concrete, salt and weather damage cause deterioration, as does overall poor construction. The risers may be unequal, too high, or too shallow. The treads may be too narrow or too wide, or open or more temporary looking than they should be. The whole system may be out of scale or have an uninteresting shape.

Repair or Rebuild?

Whether you are renovating for size, shape, or poor repair, these three problems can be attacked together with a complete face-lift or can be approached individually. For instance, if a freestanding concrete system suffers from all three problems, it may be most economical to have it removed and to install a new system that better fits your needs. If it needs repairs, but is the right size and shape, it still may be more economical to install a new system because the repairs may be more time-consuming and costly than buying a new set of steps. The best way to make this decision is by looking at all the possibilities that fall within your budget and then deciding whether to repair or build new.

There are certain renovating jobs you can tackle yourself if you have the tools and the know-how. You can lift and reset an existing stoop system that has settled. You can face or repair the facing of a freestanding unit or one that is tied into the foundation. And if you have the carpentry

Front Entry Options

A detached concrete stoop is easily covered with bluestone. Sides of the stoop and steps are stuccoed to decrease expenses. The stoop is ample enough in size to allow two people to approach the door at the same time. (Photo by Boyd Hagan; © The Taunton Press, Inc.)

This detached concrete stoop and step system has been faced with bricks. You also can start from scratch and build a masonry brick stoop with a solid footing and infrastructure. (Photo by Boyd Hagan; © The Taunton Press, Inc.)

A concrete stoop can be removed completely and a stoop of fieldstone with stacked fieldstone steps can be constructed. This is particularly appropriate for antique and Colonial style homes. (Photo by Boyd Hagan; © The Taunton Press, Inc.)

Simplicity and function are the highlights of this wooden stoop and steps. An existing attached concrete stoop, which can't be removed, could be covered with wood for a similar effect. (Photo by Charles Miller; © The Taunton Press, Inc.)

An elaborate
makeover for a free-
standing concrete
stoop system included
stone facing for the
risers and bluestone
for the treads and
stoop. Stone-faced,
decorative walls give
the entry real impor-
tance. (Photo by Charles
Bickford; © The Taunton
Press, Inc.)

skills, you can build a new wooden deck
and steps or cover an attached concrete
stoop with wood. On the other hand, if
you've never tackled a masonry or carpentry
job before, it is a good idea to leave the
work to a professional.

PREFABRICATED CONCRETE SYSTEM
The prefabricated concrete stoop and steps
system is the simplest to change. If it has
settled, it can be lifted with a machine and
placed back down on top of a new bed of
gravel that brings it to the proper height or
straightens it out. Or it can be easily

Covering a Concrete Stoop

Before

A concrete stoop and minimal foundation plantings do little to enhance the front entry.

Shrub

Concrete stoop

After

With a wood-covered stoop and renovated planting beds, the front entry is beautiful and inviting.

Curved planting bed

Wooden stoop covering old concrete stoop

Curved planting bed

How to Face a Stoop and Steps with Bluestone

1. Remove old mortar, mastic, grime, salts, and oils from the concrete surfaces with a muriatic acid wash. Follow the manufacturer's directions and wear the proper safety equipment—heavy-duty rubber gloves, eye protection, skin protection, and face mask. Thoroughly wash the acid from the area before proceeding.

2. Wet down the stoop with a hose. Mix Portland cement and water to the consistency of paste in a plastic bucket. (This is called bullock by masons and is the key to a good bond.)

3. Use a wheelbarrow and shovel to mix about 10 shovels full of sand, half a bag of Portland cement, and a little water, adding the water a bit at a time. This is the mortar mix. Its consistency should be like thick, dry peanut butter.

4. Spread bullock on the stoop where the first few stones will go. It sets up fast, so you must work quickly, especially in warm weather (see photo A).

5. Beginning with the first stone on an edge of the stoop, place mortar mix on top of the bullock where the stone will go, spreading it out an inch or so deep (see photo B).

removed the same way it arrived: with a machine, chains or crane, and a truck. It can be replaced with a prefabricated unit of a different size, shape, or step configuration or with an entirely new look—wood, brick, flat boulders, or whatever you fancy and your pocketbook will allow. It can also be faced with bricks, fieldstone, or flagstone to create a new look and cover unsightly cracks and pitting.

In warm climates, tile and other man-made materials are also used for facing. If your system is already faced, and the facing materials or grout have deteriorated, they can be removed and the surface refaced

6. Lay the stone on the mortar and use a rubber mallet to hammer it in place (see photo C). Test for evenness with a construction level, keeping an eye on the bubble of fluid that indicates the pitch. The pitch should be a little less than a quarter bubble from the back of the stoop to the front.

7. When it is pitched properly, lift up the stone and slather the bottom with bullock (see photo D). Replace the stone and hammer it again to set it. Check pitch as you go and keep the stones at the same height. Continue with all of the stones until the top of the stoop is finished. Place the stones as close together as possible, spacing them no farther apart than 1/2 in.

8. Grout the joints with a dry mortar mix (see photo E). It must be very dry, otherwise the grout will stain the stones. Test for wetness by making a ball of the mix in your hand. If it is too wet, it will stain your hand. Use a jointer to shove the grout into the joints. The joints are filled when you cannot fit any more grout in. Sweep off excess grout and let dry for 12 hours. Then wash down the stones with a hose.

(Photos by Boyd Hagan; © The Taunton Press, Inc.)

with the same type or another material. If there are only a few areas to repair, partial refacing can be done.

ATTACHED SYSTEM

An existing concrete stoop and steps that is a part of the foundation can be faced if the size and shape are acceptable, but the concrete is in poor repair or you just don't like concrete. It is also possible for a new concrete shape to be poured and tied into the existing system if you want to change the shape or size. For instance, if the stoop and steps are square or rectangular, you can change the shape to a semicircle by adding concrete onto the front, forming a half-circle and new steps. You should hire a skilled mason to augment existing concrete to ensure a good bond between the old and the new, and it's recommended that you have the stoop and steps faced with brick or flagstone to hide the bonding.

Another possibility is to cover the entire concrete unit with wood decking. This is particularly useful when you want to enlarge the stoop or change where the steps emerge from the stoop. As long as you have the space and close all the risers of the steps

Stuccoing Risers

If you don't want to go to the expense of facing the sides and risers of your stoop and steps with stone or if you want a different look, you can stucco instead. Keep in mind, though, that you cannot stucco areas that will be walked on.

1. Make a soupy mix of sand, Portland cement, and water. Trowel it on in a thin coat and let it dry for at least 30 minutes. (In moist weather, wait longer.)

2. Use a rubber or sponge floater to apply a sandpaper-like finish to the mortar. Rub over the surface with the floater until you have the desired effect.

BUILDING TO LAST

When using wood, whether to build new steps and stoops or to cover concrete, choose wood that will not rot: cedar, redwood, greenheart, teak, or pressure-treated lumber. If you use less expensive wood that doesn't repel water naturally, such as pine or hemlock, you will need to paint or stain regularly, but even with regular upkeep you will see deterioration from the elements. It's also a good idea to use a wood preservative on all woods to protect against the weather, especially if there is no roof over the front entry.

and stoop so that you can't see underneath, it's a very effective disguise.

WOODEN SYSTEM

Wooden stoops and steps are easy to make over, too. Simply remove the old and build new or replace them with a brick, flagstone, or simple concrete system. Wood is easy to remove, and its removal gives you a blank slate that's open to many design possibilities.

A new wooden front stoop and step system should be designed and built to look like a permanent part of the entry. To make it look more permanent, you can construct a railing on both sides of the steps and enclose all the risers with wood. Open treads make a step system look lighter and more temporary and are better suited to the

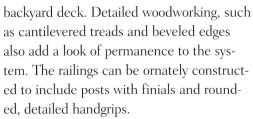

Open wooden steps look unfinished and insubstantial. They are best used for secondary entrances and decks. (Photo by Boyd Hagan; © The Taunton Press, Inc.)

Closed wooden steps give the entry a solid and finished appearance. (Photo by Maureen Gilmer.)

backyard deck. Detailed woodworking, such as cantilevered treads and beveled edges also add a look of permanence to the system. The railings can be ornately constructed to include posts with finials and rounded, detailed handgrips.

Pay careful attention to the girth of the wood you use. Use chunky, thicker wood for posts, treads, spindles, and handrails. Even though the entry is outside your home, it should be given the same attention to detail and workmanship as the kitchen cabinets.

10 Well-Designed Walkways and Patios

After you have decided what to do about your front stoop and steps, you must turn your attention to the walkway. Whether straight or curved, stone, concrete, or brick, the walkway that leads to your front door should be welcoming and safe to traverse. In this chapter, you will learn about the design and building of walkways and patios. You may decide to augment your existing walk or patio, or you may decide to start over. Either way, well-designed walkways and patios are good investments that add beauty and value to your home.

The author's walkway received a full makeover because it had an inadequate base, causing a multitude of problems year-round. A new base and realignment of stones created a safe, attractive walkway. (Photo by Judi Rutz; © The Taunton Press, Inc.)

Hidden Dangers

When, for the first time, I traversed the walkway of my new home in late fall, the neat, seemingly well-laid bluestones looked like they had been in place for a while. They were laid in a simple pattern and one that I, as a professional, could find little fault with. They seemed to be graded properly so that each stone met the next without interruption or bump. I will even go so far to say I surmised that the walkway had been installed by a professional.

What the future held can only be described as a nightmare, and it didn't take more than the first freezing temperatures to start the process. The walkway heaved and cracked with each freeze/thaw cycle and became dangerous. This was during a winter with El Niño, which raised our temperatures and our bluestone. My 84-year-old mother was its first and last (thank heaven) victim: She tripped on a heaved piece of bluestone the night before my wedding and fell flat on her back. The accident resulted in a compression fracture of her shoulder and two weeks of hospitalization from pneumonia from the resultant inactivity. Now, you have to understand, my mother is not feeble. Before the accident, she played golf every day. The walkway was so bad, this could have happened to anyone.

The culprit, in this case, was an improperly installed walkway. My guess is that it was the work of the former homeowner, who didn't know any better and installed it in

The author's walkway received a makeover of bluestone. (Photo by Boyd Hagan; © The Taunton Press, Inc.)

The author's walkway originally had small stones and large joints. (Photo by Boyd Hagan; © The Taunton Press, Inc.)

the spring with the hope of selling his house faster with an improved front entry. We happened along in the fall and were the first people to live with this walkway during the winter. The serious mistake that he made was laying the bluestone directly on the virgin soil with only about an inch of base beneath them, a method suitable for the most southern parts of the U.S., but not the rest of the country.

The moral of this story is don't be fooled by what you see on top, and even a professional can be duped. A proper base is the key to a walkway or patio that will withstand the test of time and, 10 years later, look the same as it did the day it was installed.

Anatomy of a Walkway or Patio

The first step to walkway or patio renovation is to assess what you have. There are two basic kinds of problems with patios and walkways: those associated with design and those associated with installation. Design problems are pretty obvious because they are aboveground: The walkway may be too narrow, too close to the house, too straight, or made of a material you don't like. The patio may be too small, or the shape may be unimaginative. Some installation problems—such as heaving, cracking, or weeds growing through—are obvious, but their cause is below ground. In order to correct these problems, you must know what to look for and understand the anatomy of a walkway or patio.

BASE BASICS

If you haven't lived with the walkway through a winter, you should check out what is underneath it. No matter where you live or what your patio or walkway is made of, there should be some sort of a base under it. Even poured concrete sidewalks must have a base beneath them. If you see heaving or cracked pavers, your problem is probably an inadequate base.

Lift up some bricks or stones and check out the base with a shovel or dig next to your walkway. The base should be anywhere from 4 in. to 1 ft. deep (the colder the climate, the deeper the base), and it should extend beyond the width of the walk by 4 in. to 6 in. This is so the edges and edging material do not heave when the adjacent soil freezes and thaws.

In other words, all the soil in the cavity below the paving material and to the sides of the paving material (to a maximum of 6 in.) should have been removed and replaced with a good-packing gravel base,

one comprised of several sizes of aggregate from ¾-in. pebbles to stone dust (aka rock fines), not sand and not clean, washed stone. There may be an inch of coarse sand or stone dust directly under the pavers just to bed them, but below that inch should be several inches of the aggregate gravel.

A base made strictly of sand or washed gravel never packs, and although it may not heave, the paving material will move on the

The best packing base material contains gravel mixed with smaller stone and stone dust (bottom). Stone dust is used as a bedding for bluestone and fieldstone (top left). Coarse sand (top right) is used as bedding for brick or concrete pavers. (Photo by Sloan Howard; © The Taunton Press, Inc.)

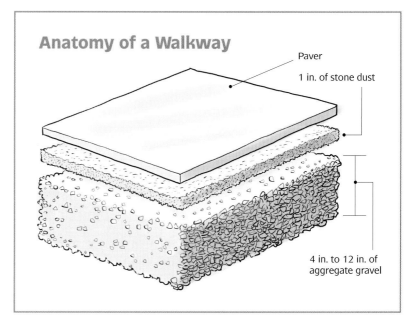

Anatomy of a Walkway

Paver

1 in. of stone dust

4 in. to 12 in. of aggregate gravel

mushy sand or gravel every time it is walked on and will appear uneven—raised in some places, sunken in others. It is also important that the hole, which is filled with the gravel, be properly graded *before* the gravel is put in it. I have fixed a patio that was completely uneven due to bricks sinking over the whole surface. When we dug up the base, we discovered that the bottom of the hole looked exactly like the top of the patio, which had mirrored its unevenness.

The base, no matter how deep, must be compacted in layers during the backfill. A plate compactor is used to vibrate the particles, which packs them together. This process cannot be overdone. If the paving material has sunk in areas, it may be because the base was not compacted well

enough. The only solution, unfortunately, is to remove all the pavers, compact the base well, and relay the surface.

Common Problems

You may have a walkway that has weeds growing between the pavers, or perhaps you have a concrete walkway or patio with cracks. Or you may not be happy with the material, shape, or size of your walkway or patio. Sometimes these systems can be saved without ripping them out and starting again.

WEEDY WALKWAYS

A good walkway base will provide a sterile material, free of nutrients and weed seeds, so that grass and weeds will not grow between pavers. When weed seeds are dropped by birds or blown in, they are easily removed by hand pulling. But if weeds are impossible to pull without leaving the roots behind, there is a good chance the base material is soil or was not sterile to begin with.

If the walkway hasn't been weeded in ages, the weeds will be hard to pull, in which case the base may not be to blame. The weeds' roots may have matured under

A plate compactor is used to pack base materials. It is run over the surface as each layer is added.
(Photo by Susan Kahn;
© The Taunton Press, Inc.)

A CASUAL WALKWAY
Create a casual walkway from individual paving stones, sections of tree trunks, or tiles laid directly on the soil if you are building the walkway through a woodland or garden that is used only during the summer. Because this walkway is not maintained or used when freezing or thawing is occurring, it doesn't require a base.

the paving stones. When you pull them, you will leave the roots behind, and the weeds will grow right back. Your best bet is to apply a nonresidual systemic herbicide, such as Round-Up. This chemical is so safe that it is prescribed for use near watersheds because it does not reside in the soil. It attacks the plant through its leaves and travels down its system to the roots, killing the whole plant without contaminating the environment.

CRACKED CONCRETE

You may see hairline or larger cracks in concrete, or the facing material or grout may be cracked. This is usually due to an inadequate base or settling of the base after the paving material was installed. If the concrete has been in place for a long time, it probably has done all the settling it is going to do, and if the cracks are hairline, you may choose to live with them. If the cracks continuously get worse, however, the concrete should be removed and the base rebuilt and

compacted. If the concrete is faced with stone or brick, you should fix the base and concrete before you fix the facing material. Don't repair facing material and grout without first fixing the concrete and base beneath—it is a waste of time and money.

DESIGN FAULTS

Even if the walkway or patio was installed properly, you may be tired of the shape, the size may be inadequate for your present needs, the paving material may be in poor repair, or you may not like the paving material. It is possible, under certain circumstances, to augment an existing walkway or patio without starting over, which I will describe later. First you must decide on a new design, taking into consideration the limitations presented by using the existing walkway or patio and integrating it with your new ideas, which should be influenced by basic design principles.

Although fieldstone may not be a good choice for the main walkway because of its irregularities, it is a fine choice for woodland paths and other secondary walks. Ground covers grown in the joints soften the harshness of the stone and make it particularly inviting. (Photo by Delilah Smittle; © The Taunton Press, Inc.)

Surface Materials

On top of the gravel base lies the paving material: poured concrete; poured concrete faced with flagstone or brick; or a dry laid surface of brick, flagstone, bluestone, field-stone, precast concrete pavers, or any other manufactured paving stone. In cold climates, it is not advisable to use any paving material that is not specified for outdoor use. Old brick from a fireplace, for example, will not withstand freezing and thawing cycles and will crumble and crack. If you see deterioration with bricks, there is a good chance the proper bricks were not used. There are specially made brick pavers for outdoor use, which have additives to strengthen them.

You can also use precast concrete pavers, which come in many shapes, sizes, and colors. They are specially made for outdoor paving and are extremely versatile for walkways and patios. The installation is the same as for bricks, but their durability is unsurpassed by any material for home use other than asphalt. Some precast concrete pavers can withstand as much as 2,000 pounds per square inch of weight, which means you can drive on and snowplow them.

If you're thinking about using natural stone as a paving material, keep in mind that it has fissures and irregularities. You must decide if it is appropriate for the area in which it will be used. For example, field-stone is probably not the best material for a swimming pool patio where people will be walking bare-footed because this material is uneven and absorbs heat.

If the natural stone you are considering plates and chips beyond what you can tolerate, you should avoid using it as paving material. There are geologic regions with unstable stone, so you should check with local masonry suppliers to find stone that is stable in your region. Slate, which readily plates, is not a good choice for paving, and it can be quite slippery when wet. Natural stone also can pit and deteriorate from de-icing salts, and you may have to avoid using salt if you want to use a certain stone.

Proper Pitch

For water to shed off a walkway or patio, there must be 1 in. of pitch in 8 ft. of distance. Patios and walkways should also pitch from side to side. How much and which way is determined by the width of the walkway or patio and where you want water to flow. Obviously, it must flow away from the foundation of the house, but it

Properly Pitched Walkway

A curved walkway may have to be pitched (1 in. in 8 ft.) in two or more directions to move water efficiently.

may pitch in more than one direction to accomplish that. If you have water puddling on the walkway or patio, use a transit or handheld level to figure out if there is any pitch at all or whether there are actually dips within the walkway or patio. To fix the problem, you must remove the paving surface and build up the base accordingly until the transit reads that there is adequate pitch for water to move or that the dips are gone.

The Well-Designed Walkway

The main walkway to the front door should create a lasting impression on your guests. All secondary walkways should blend into the rest of the landscaping, but still be safe and functional. Safety and function are established with proper grading, good surface materials, and adequate lighting, whereas good impressions are created by shape, color, and size.

Aesthetically, the main walkway should be at least 4 ft. wide to allow two people to walk together side by side. It can flare out to meet the stoop or meet it straight on, but either way, it should flare out at the other end where it meets the driveway or sidewalk. This creates a friendly, inviting entry to your home. The main walkway is best laid sweeping away from the house, leaving a space for plantings between the walk and house walls. This also allows a perspective view of the house as your guests approach the front door. The walkway can be straight or curved. I prefer to soften the geometric lines of the house by curving the walkway where it bends rather than echoing the lines of the house with angles. A curving walkway should still bring you to the front door without going too far out of your way, otherwise it will be bypassed in favor of a beeline.

Secondary walkways are often used when there are two doors on the front of your house or to move from one side of the

A well-designed walkway is splayed at the end where it meets the drive or street for an inviting entry. It is wide enough to accommodate two people walking side by side, and it is pulled away from house walls to allow for plantings. (Photo by Kathleen Kolb.)

A Tale of Two Front Entries

It is common to have more than one front entry, one used by the family and the larger, more prominent one used by guests. I have been at homes, however, where the main front door is never used, and I suggest if you are in that camp, you don't spend too much time deliberating about fixing it up—it probably doesn't need much fixing.

Nevertheless, no matter which door you intend guests to use, designing the spaces so they are used the way you want requires some of these tricks of the trade.

• **Draw attention.** Whichever door you want guests to use should draw their attention. This means building a larger deck or stoop at the threshold, stretching it beyond the width of the door. At least two people should be able to stand on it and not be pushed off by an opening door.

The walkway to the primary entry should be wider, and the secondary walkway should either branch off of it or be detached from it. The primary walkway should be splayed at the end where it meets the driveway or sidewalk to make it more inviting than the secondary walk. It is a good idea to sweep it away from the house face, so guests get glimpses of the front door as they approach it.

• **Use plantings as focal points.** Plantings, designed to provide focal points of color or shape along the path, will guide your guests to the correct door. Warm-colored flowers, such as reds and yellows, will draw the eye and, by night, lighting that highlights those plants will create the focus.

• **Minimize the secondary entry.** To minimize the impact of the secondary entry, build a smaller stoop, narrow the walkway, or change the surface material to distinguish it from the main walkway. Use a common rather than intricate pattern of pavers or brick or simply use packed, crushed stone for the smaller walk. Create a jog or interruption in the path of the secondary walkway, such as a plant that people must step around, to force guests to go out of their way to use it. Chances are, they won't.

• **Use roadblocks.** Block the view of the secondary walkway with plants or low fencing. An island planting between the two walkways will take the secondary path out of the line of sight. Even a hedge of evergreens can be used, if needed. Use cool-colored flowers that recede from your eye and, if all else fails, turn off the lights associated with that entry when you are expecting guests.

There is no question which front entry should be used when an island bed is used to separate the walkways. It also shields the secondary entry from view. (Photo by Sara Jane von Trapp; © The Taunton Press, Inc.)

A secondary walkway to the mudroom is narrower and masked by plantings. (Photo by Kathleen Kolb.)

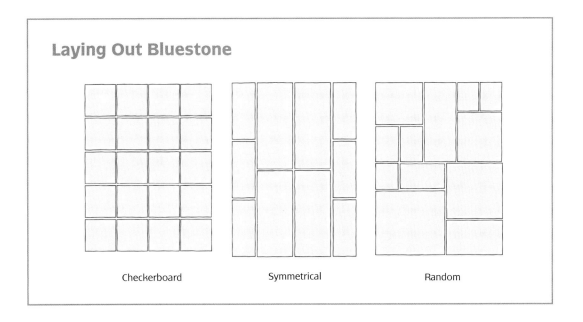

Laying Out Bluestone

Checkerboard   Symmetrical   Random

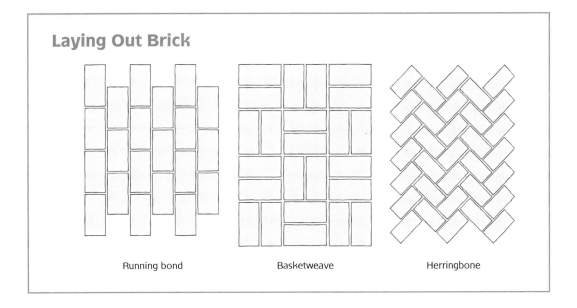

Laying Out Brick

Running bond   Basketweave   Herringbone

house to another without walking on the grass. They can be minimal, such as simple stepping stones, or they can be bona fide walkways, minimized (as described in "A Tale of Two Front Entries") to discourage visitors from using them or to diminish their intrusion on the landscape.

CHOOSING PAVING MATERIALS

When choosing paving materials for walks, you should take into consideration degree of formality (which may be dictated by the purpose of the walk), house color and paving colors, and ease of maintenance.

Formality

Main walkways are usually more formal than secondary walkways. Formality can be created with pattern design and color. For instance, plain concrete works fine for a secondary walkway, but you may want to face it with red brick for the front-door walk. If both are brick, you can use an intricate herringbone pattern for the front walk

A meandering, ample bluestone walkway with muted tones blends with the house architecture and landscaping. (Photo by Kathleen Kolb.)

bluestone or flagstone, which have blue-grays and pinks in their color range—are eastern stones. I prefer to use indigenous stone regardless of house color because I think it blends with the local landscape better, but you can import stone to match house or door color if you wish.

Maintenance

If you live in snow country, you need to consider this maintenance issue. If you use a snowblower or snowplow, you will need a durable surface like concrete that can take the abuse. Shovelers can use just about any surface, but it should be continuous to avoid bone-rattling collisions with the edges of rocks. You need not be as concerned about the surfaces of secondary walkways that will not be used during the winter, and therefore, not maintained during the winter. Areas that will be used only during summer months can include ground covers between paving stones and more irregular surfaces.

Weeds are another maintenance concern. As discussed earlier, with the proper base, weeds should not pose a problem, no matter what the surface. If you plan on a gravel walk without a paving material on top, you will want to use a sheet of myrify fabric (weed cloth) under the gravel, so that weeds from below will not grow through.

and a toned-down, simple running bond for the walkway to the back. Materials like concrete pavers and natural stone are less formal than brick, and aggregate gravel or stone dust is the least formal.

Color

Brick is available in several colors from reds to tans, including blends of colors. Precast concrete pavers run the gamut from pinks, grays, tans, and browns to less natural-looking blends of these colors. Natural stone is usually subdued in color. Fieldstone color varies from region to region. Gray granite, white marble, and dark gray shales predominate in the eastern U.S., and pink and yellow sandstone can be found in the western states. Quarried stone—such as

Building a Walkway

As I related earlier in this chapter, the walkway I inherited had become unsightly and unsafe (see pp. 134-135 for how my bluestone walkway was renovated). While you may not have identical problems to correct, this will give you a good idea of the work involved in building a walkway.

The Well-Designed Patio

Design of walkways and patios are similar, differing only in size and shape. You are not restricted to square lines and angles because paving materials and the equipment used to install them have been developed to accommodate curves. When it comes to designing a patio, you are restricted only by your imagination and how much space you have in your yard.

SIZE

If you need to renovate the patio because it is too small, you can decide on the proper size by drawing it, as is, on paper. Measure your outdoor furniture, too, and make scale models of the furniture to set up on your drawing. Make sure you leave enough space for pulling out chairs around a dining table, working in front of the barbecue, walking around chaise lounges, and walking across the patio to the yard. As you augment the drawing to accommodate the furniture, a shape and size will start to gel.

If a free-form shape isn't your style, make the shape into one that is more recognizable, like a rectangle, oval, or kidney. Keep in mind that curved shapes make use of all available space, while rectangles and squares have empty corners. If you wish to have angles, you are better off using the empty corners for chair pullouts or steps to

This well-designed patio is constructed of precast concrete pavers shaped especially to form a perfect circle. Its design is the perfect fit for the Victorian house and informal country setting. (Photo © Alden Pellet.)

Building a Walkway Step-by-Step

Removing the old walkway revealed an inadequate base below. The old stones were laid aside for reuse. (Photo by Boyd Hagan; © The Taunton Press, Inc.)

The machine couldn't reach the top level of the walkway, so it was dug out by hand. At least 8 in. of soil was removed. (Photo by Boyd Hagan; © The Taunton Press, Inc.)

The lower part of the walkway was excavated using a skid-steer loader. The machine removes a swath the exact width of the walkway plus an extra 4 in. on each side. (Photo by Boyd Hagan; © The Taunton Press, Inc.)

To keep the edge of the stones in the finished walkway from heaving, the ground was dug out 4 in. wider than the finished walkway. Hand tools were used to keep lawn damage to a minimum. (Photo by Boyd Hagan; © The Taunton Press, Inc.)

The excavated walkway was filled with gravel, leaving room for 1 in. of bedding (either rock fines or coarse sand) and the width of the bluestone. (Photo by Boyd Hagan; © The Taunton Press, Inc.)

A plate compactor was used to fully compact the gravel base. This is done in layers of a few inches of gravel at a time by running the machine over the surface again and again. (Photo by Boyd Hagan; © The Taunton Press, Inc.)

The workers use a line stretched along the edge to keep their work straight. Bluestone pieces are then fit together and leveled in the bedding stone dust. (Photo by Boyd Hagan; © The Taunton Press, Inc.)

A few taps from a rubber mallet made the joints very tight. A construction level was used to ensure that the stones were level from side to side and pitched forward for the length of the walkway. (Photo by Boyd Hagan; © The Taunton Press, Inc.)

Coarse sand was swept in to fill the joints. The final piece of bluestone was then chosen and cut to fit in the remaining space. (Photo by Boyd Hagan; © The Taunton Press, Inc.)

More stone dust was added frequently beneath the bluestone pieces to properly bed and level them. (Photo by Boyd Hagan; © The Taunton Press, Inc.)

The final piece was put in place. (Photo by Boyd Hagan; © The Taunton Press, Inc.)

A fieldstone patio is made with wide enough joints to grow ground covers in between the stones. This patio is not maintained in the winter so the wide joints and plants pose no danger to pedestrians. (Photo by Kathleen Kolb.)

another level or making the angles mimic curving spaces—like a hexagon—to open them up.

MATERIALS

As with secondary walkways, paving materials are usually less formal for a patio. If you don't mind moving your chair around to find good footing, you can use natural stone with irregularities or plant ground covers between stones for informality. In this setting, you can be more carefree about pattern and color of your paving materials.

The Possibilities for Change

You've learned about the anatomy of walkways and patios and what generally can go wrong with them. Now you must decide if it is worth the time and money to fix the problems or if it is better to start over. If the basic structure is sound, but the design doesn't suit your lifestyle or taste, it is usually possible to change the look or size without starting from scratch. If the walkway or patio is

constructed of concrete, you can face it with brick or flagstone or build a border around it out of another material to make it larger and more attractive. If you want to change the shape or increase the size of a patio, you can add on at the same level or add another level to the existing patio.

FACING

As with concrete stoops and steps, you can face a concrete walkway or patio with brick or natural stone. The procedures are the same, but the area is larger, which makes the project a bigger deal. You cannot do it in parts, so a chunk of time is needed to complete the job. You may decide to have a professional do the facing work.

MAKING A BORDER

A simpler way to dress up concrete is to make a border along the edges with dry-laid brick, pavers, or stone. This is especially effective if your walkway isn't as wide as you'd like it to be because you can kill two birds with one stone: You can make it wider and more attractive simultaneously.

To make a border with mortared brick or stone, you must first pour a base of concrete and insert metal ties between the old concrete and the new. The base will be lower, by the thickness of the brick or stone, than the existing surface. In cold climates, this is risky without a footing to stabilize the base. It is a much less expensive job to augment with dry-laid borders. Here are the basic steps for adding a border.

Step 1: Dig a hole for a base next to the walkway on both sides, 4 in. to 6 in. wider than the finished width. Use the concrete as the straight edge on the inside and plastic or aluminum edging on the outside. If the border is around a patio, you will be augmenting the outside edge of the patio.

Step 2: Install the edging, then the base and bedding material, and compact well in between each layer. Leave space for your paving surface, which will be the thickness of the pavers, bricks, or stone. Lay precast concrete pavers about ¼ in. higher than the finished height, so they can be tamped down into the bedding sand to match the level of the existing concrete. None of the other paving surfaces can be run over with a plate compactor, so they should be figured at finished height.

ADDING TO THE PATIO

One way to augment an existing patio that is too small is to add a new level of space a step or so down or to add on a shape to the existing area on the same level. The advantage to having different levels is that you

A poured concrete walkway is dressed up with an edge of pre-cast concrete pavers and an adjacent pre-cast concrete paver secondary walkway.
(Photo by Kathleen Kolb.)

PVC edging is installed before the pavers to hold them in place. Note the string line used to keep a straight, square edge.
(Photo by Susan Kahn;
© The Taunton Press, Inc.)

Edging Options

Running Bond Edge

The simplest pattern to use with brick is a running bond, and you can make it as wide as you want. A typical 3-ft.-wide concrete walkway looks well with an edge on both sides that is two or three brick widths wide. That way there is no cutting involved except possibly at either end of the walkway.

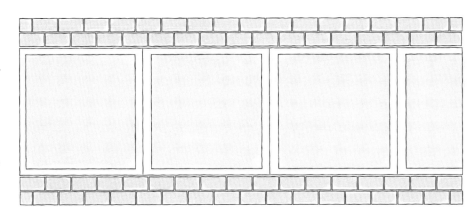

Basketweave Edge

You could also edge with one width of basketweave pattern. If you are using natural stone like bluestone or flagstone, buy precut pieces, 6 in. to 12 in. wide and at least 12 in. long, and run them in a line along the edge(s) of the walk or patio.

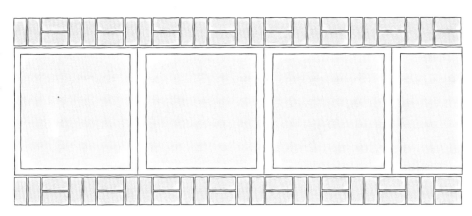

Brick Edge

You can use even wider stone or several bricks, pavers, or stones for the edge of a patio, but keep the edge in scale with the existing patio. You will be surprised at how a border like this dresses up a walkway or patio.

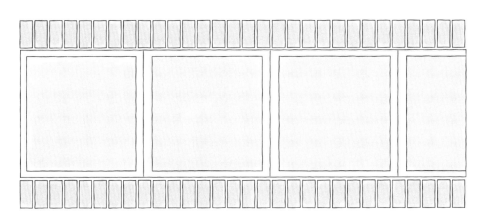

can easily separate the uses of the two levels. For instance, the upper level can be used for dining and barbecuing, while the lower level can be for sitting and sunning.

If you have decided to build a level on your patio out of dry-laid brick, pavers, or stone, the job is similar to adding a border, but the scale is bigger. You'll need a machine to dig the base and will also have to pay careful attention to grade and pitch.

I recommend you get an estimate from a pro before you take on the project to see if it is worth your effort. Yes, you will save money doing it yourself, but you do not want to do this job twice if it doesn't come out right the first time. To make the cost seem more reasonable, consider your existing patio an asset and spread the cost over the entire square footage, old and new.

A mortared patio is an even bigger deal because you need to pour footings and a slab of concrete and then face the concrete. If you are trying to match an existing patio,

it's the way to go. You'll want the addition to be tied into the existing patio, so that they move together with freezing and thawing. Otherwise, a gap may develop. If the new area is at a different level, you can tie the two together with pressure-treated timbers, granite curbing, or a concrete curb.

Lighting: The Finishing Touch

Once you've renovated or replaced your walkways and patio, you can enhance your landscape with good lighting. Task lighting is important along walkways to keep them safe.

Ornamental low-voltage lamps for pathway lighting are available in copper and brass as well as black and green aluminum. In addition to providing light for walkways and patios, these task lights can also provide downlighting for stairways and decks. (For more on lighting, see pp. 163-165.)

A two-level free-form patio makes the space more interesting and steps the land down gradually. The different spaces are divided for dining and relaxing near the pool. (Photo by Kathleen Kolb.)

11 Transforming an Old Deck

I think a deck is one of the most important living spaces you have. In the two houses I have owned, I have used my decks year-round for barbecuing, dining, sunning, gardening, and winding down at the end of the day.

Dare to be different and change that old unimaginative deck to a masterpiece like this redwood creation. The wood is impressive by itself but add curves, ample stairs, and interesting rails and you have a work of art! (Photo by Marvin Sloben; courtesy California Redwood Association.)

The author's Vermont deck is curved and free-form, fitting the country setting and informality of the house and surroundings. The deck flows naturally through the landscape, tying it to the earth. (Photo © Alden Pellet.)

I had the luxury of building my first deck from scratch so I was able to design and build it just as I wanted. It was elaborate and elegant—round with curved railings, entry boardwalks, and chunky structural components that made it look and feel solid. It had two access points so you didn't have to walk around the house to go from one side of the house to the other. The railing design was simple and fashioned so that when you were seated and the railing was at eye level, it did not obstruct the view of the sunsets over Lake Champlain and the Adirondack Mountains. You could set a drink on the flat, spacious rail without it tumbling to the ground, and there were separate seating areas—one for dining and one for whiling away the hours gazing at that view.

I remember that deck with great yearning because with my new house I've inherited a deck without any of those features. My new deck is spacious, but it is an unimaginative rectangle with an ugly, obtrusive railing that won't hold a drink, and you feel jailed-in when you are seated and trying to look beyond to the lovely, wooded view. The deck has only one access point, so you have to walk around the entire house to mount the stairs. I couldn't wait to make it more usable and more attractive.

If you, too, are living with a deck that is not suited to your needs, don't despair. It is relatively easy to change and augment a deck. The first step is to take an assessment of your present deck.

Start with What You Have

Before you begin to plan changes to your deck, you must determine if it is structurally sound. Hire a licensed builder to check for rot and deterioration. The builder will look at all the components, including the support posts in the ground. The builder will also be able to tell you what your deck can support in the way of changes without you having to go to too much expense to beef it up.

Familiarize yourself with any regulations your town may impose concerning decks. Town regulations may restrict what can be done with heights of railings, stairways, depths of support posts, size of support beams, distance between spindles, and removal of railings. And don't forget that you will need to get a building permit before you begin your renovations.

Designing the Changes

You probably know what parts of your deck you would like to change. The best way to begin is to sketch your ideas on paper. Then, if you have the know-how, you can determine what materials you need and how much it will cost to build in the changes. If you don't understand the infrastructure of building a deck, you can ask for estimates from a few builders to determine who you would like to work with, but first you will need the drawing.

Draw your existing deck from a bird's-eye view, including the wall(s) of the house to which it is attached. Also make some scaled-down versions of your deck furniture and grill, which you can move around on the drawing to try different arrangements. Use a piece of tracing paper over the drawing of the existing deck to try out additions to the deck.

SHAPE

Don't feel locked into the current dimensions of the deck. For instance, I planned to attach another level to my existing deck that is a step down and offset from the existing structure. It hangs over by 8 ft. and only reaches halfway across the existing deck. Creating two levels and offsetting the two rectangular decks is more interesting than just tacking on an adjacent piece. Even if your existing deck is rectangular, you are not locked into adding on an identically shaped section, especially if the new section is at a different level. The new section can be curved, geometric, or square.

LEVELS

Many people have an elevated deck with dead space underneath. They are tired of looking at the underside of the deck. When you add on a section at a lower level, you can build as many steps as are needed in between the decks to get you closer to ground level. The steps can stretch the entire length of the step-down to really open up the new space to the old. The transition to the ground is more gradual, and the new level provides additional dining and recreation space.

ACCESS

Access to the yard from the deck is an important consideration. If the deck is small, stairs can be centrally located and one set may be adequate. However, when a

Rounded edges and a bridge over landscaping makes this deck a functional, attractive area with several seating and dining possibilities. (Photo by Delilah Smittle; © The Taunton Press, Inc.)

deck stretches the entire length of the house or around a corner, you will want more than one access area. It is a small job to cut a hole in the railing and add another set of steps, but it will make a big difference in convenience for your family.

HOT TUBS

Many people improve a deck by adding a hot tub. If this is something you'd like to do, plan for it in your design. When you draw your deck design, be sure to leave enough space to walk around the tub, get in and out of it, and hang around near it. You can be creative about access to the equipment panels on the side of the tub, and a trap door in the floor of the deck is one way to handle the problem. Your builder needs to pay attention to structural support for the huge weight your deck must bear.

Before remodeling, the author's deck had a jail-like railing and unimaginative shape. (Photo by Boyd Hagan; © The Taunton Press, Inc.)

The railing was removed and benches and planters were added in its place. Two levels with wide stairs create separate spaces and an attractive terrace to the ground. (Photo by Judi Rutz; © The Taunton Press, Inc.)

Dealing with Dead Space

You can close up the underside of an elevated deck to hide its unsightliness without adding on a new level. One way is to use lattice to cover the open space. Prefabricated lattice is available, or you can build lattice to any dimension. The lattice can then be covered with a flowering vine to break up the monotony.

Another option for the dead space under the deck is complete closure. Since I have never been partial to lattice under decks, on my first deck in Vermont I closed up the underside with horizontal skirt boards where the deck was only 30 in. off the ground, and I made a closet underneath to store seasonal items where it was higher off the ground. I made the closet by attaching a hinged door within the skirt boards.

A third option is to plant a layered bed to hide the dead space underneath the deck, as illustrated below.

No matter what you do to hide that dead space, you will greatly improve the look of your deck.

(Photo by Rich Ziegner; © The Taunton Press, Inc.)

A Layered Bed Hides Dead Space

Use layered plantings to hide the space left below an elevated deck.

A trellis over the deck is a great way to dress it up. Plants climb and twist around the wood to offer shade and color during the growing season. (Photo by Marvin Sloben; courtesy California Redwood Association.)

Imaginative, accessible steps and a hot tub improved this deck that now functions like an outdoor room. (Photo by Bruce Greenlaw; © The Taunton Press, Inc.)

Cosmetic Changes

The simplest way to improve an old deck is to paint or stain it. Or, you can give it a "seaside" look by bleaching the wood. Ordinary household bleach, in a solution of equal parts water and bleach, can be brushed on to create a graying effect. If that effect is too subtle for you, bleach oil or commercial wood bleach can be applied according to the manufacturer's suggestions. Keep in mind that sometimes it takes a good six months to get the full effect of bleaching.

The Details

Once you've determined the big elements, like size, shape, and levels, it's time to move on to the nitty-gritty details that make a deck more inviting.

RAILINGS

You can add new interest to an old deck by changing the railings or adding details to the existing railings. You can even remove the railings and use built-in planters and/or benches to delineate the space. Be sure that you check your town regulations to see if this is permissible. Your town may have regulations that require installation of full-fledged railings on decks that are above a certain height.

One way to dress up a railing is to change the posts holding up the railing sections and replace them with posts that have interesting tops or finials.

Another way to dress up a railing is to remove the railing sections and replace them with another material. This may be done to take advantage of a view, block the

Planters and benches instead of railings keep this deck safe as a house-to-pool go-between. (Photo by Boyd Hagan; © The Taunton Press, Inc.)

Railing Styles

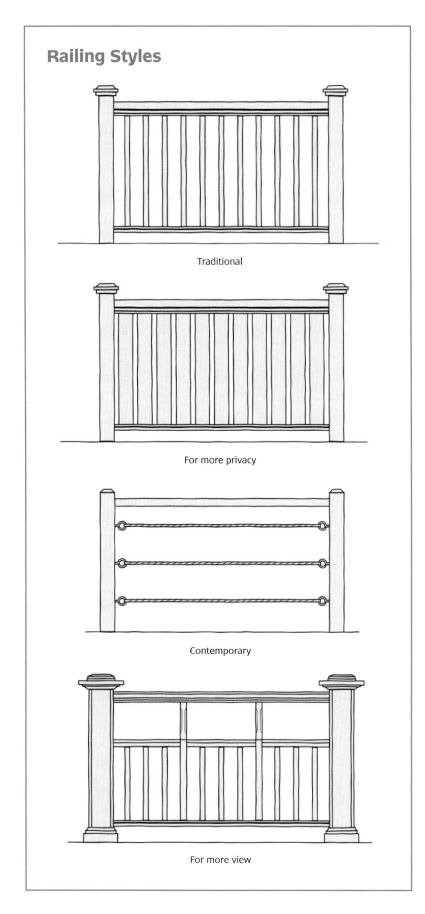

Traditional

For more privacy

Contemporary

For more view

wind by using clear Plexiglas panels, or make the rail more solid for privacy. For more privacy, lattice is an effective screen, as is a fencelike stockade wall.

There are several styles for railings, both simple and elaborate. One of the best ways to decide what to install on your deck is to drive around and look at other people's railings. Personal preference comes into play. I like a flat, wide handrail to set a drink or window box on and simple 2-in. by 2-in. spindles that end a few inches up from the deck floor, attached to another horizontal member. The opening allows you to sweep the deck without obstruction.

SHADING

You can create a new look for your deck by shading it. Colorful awnings are expensive, but they are effective and easy to stretch out or fold up if you don't want to block the light. Awning companies offer several designs, including one that opens and closes at the push of a button.

Building a shade structure, arbor, or trellis over your deck is a great way to dress it up. The shade structure can be covered with canvas, lathe, mesh shade cloth, or any shading material. It can be attached to the house or freestanding. If the deck is at ground level, you can grow vines to climb up the posts and shade the deck with their growth. On an elevated deck, fast-growing annual vines, such as morning glory or pole beans, can be grown in containers, or, in warm climates, perennial vines will survive in containers. Whichever option you prefer, first check with your builder to make sure your deck and house can support the weight a shade structure may add.

LIGHTING

Lighting is another way to change the look of an old deck. Ornamental outdoor fixtures can be attached to posts, and wiring can be

An awning not only shades the deck but provides an attractive, colorful accent. It can create a whole new look for your deck. (Photo courtesy Otter Creek Awnings and Patio Rooms.)

easily hidden under handrail caps. The cap is removed and a groove is carved on the underside to carry the wire before the rail is reattached.

Low-voltage lighting, which tends to be less ornamental, is also available specifically for decks. A string of tiny lights set about 1 ft. apart is attached under the handrail cap to delineate where the end of the deck is after dark. Stair risers and railing posts also can be fitted with recessed lights, which are the size of electric outlet covers. Don't be fooled by the size of these lights; low-voltage lighting can be powerful, yet it is economical. (Your car's headlights are low-voltage lamps.)

The key to low-voltage lighting is not overtaxing the wattage limits. If a string of low-voltage lights allows 100 watts, you must only use 80 percent of the wattage to ensure there will be no voltage drop or dimming of the lights at the end of the string.

The beauty of low-voltage lighting is that you are not paying for high-priced fixtures. The fixtures are placed out of sight so you see only the light—the essential feature. Your deck will be lit up for beauty and safety and will remain the focal point in the scheme.

Low-voltage lighting dresses up an old deck. It is the light that is emphasized, not the fixtures, and the effect is not only utilitarian but also elegant. (Photo courtesy Hadco.)

12 The Yard beyond the House

As you complete your landscaping plan, you will want to include yard spaces beyond the house, such as a pool or water feature, play areas, outlying gardens, and work areas. With your landscaped spaces carefully planned, not only will all the areas in your yard be integrated, but nothing will appear to be an afterthought.

The yard beyond the house includes perennial borders, vegetable gardens, shady sitting areas, and a pool. Yours may have a play area, a pond, a water garden, or a gazebo. (Photo © The Taunton Press, Inc.)

Adding a Pool

Until recently, my experience with pool projects has been as the landscape designer and contractor who cleans up the aftermath in someone else's yard. I have spent hours helping homeowners locate the pool, tie it in to existing patios and decks, pick out fencing, and beautify the space with shrubs and flowers. Doing it in my own yard has been harder than any other project I have ever done, and experiencing the day-to-day ups and downs, noise and dirt, and decision making has been a real eye-opener. I hope that by recounting my experience, I can help you anticipate what you are getting into and help you avoid making costly mistakes.

The author's new pool added to an old yard.
(Photo by Boyd Hagan; © The Taunton Press, Inc.)

TOWN REGULATIONS

Find out what the setback regulations are in your area because they could have a major impact on your pool siting. In my town, I found out that the pool itself (not including fencing and decking) must be 40 ft. from the property line and 25 ft. from all parts of the septic system—tank, distribution boxes, and lines. These setback numbers vary from state to state and town to town, but it gives you a rough idea of what you may run into.

Trees are marked for removal with red flagging. Only three are directly in the path of the pool; others are removed to open up the site to more sun. (Photo by Boyd Hagan; © The Taunton Press, Inc.)

Trees have been removed and the site is ready for laying out the pool. (Photo by Boyd Hagan; © The Taunton Pres, Inc.)

BUDGET FIRST

The first step in planning a pool is to create a realistic budget. There are many factors to consider when developing this:

- Where are the property lines, and what are the setback regulations in your town?
- Where is the septic system (tank, distribution boxes, and lines) and well? Or, in a municipality, where are the pipes leading into the house?
- Are there trees in the way of the pool or trees that will cast shade on the pool?
- Is there a place to bury stumps and rocks or must they be trucked away?
- What are the zoning regulations regarding fences?
- Do you want a vinyl-lined or concrete pool?
- What shape and size pool will fit?
- How will you tie in the pool to the existing features in the yard?
- What kind of pool cover do you want?
- What kind of surface do you want surrounding the pool?
- Will you build an enclosure for the pump and filter system (with changing space) or just pour a concrete pad for it and disguise it with plants?
- What type of fencing do you want?
- How much lawn and landscape work will you need?

You will need help answering these questions. Your best resources are town administrators, pool contractors, fencing contractors, arborists, and landscape contractors. In my case, I spoke with four different pool contractors who came to my house, looked over the site, and were familiar with the regulations in my town. Knowing your town regulations during the budgetary process is necessary because permits cost money, you may need to take down trees, or you may need to get a variance (legal permission to build outside of the setback regulations), which can also cost money.

A concrete pool with bluestone coping is expensive but elegant.
(Photo by Boyd Hagan; © The Taunton Press, Inc.)

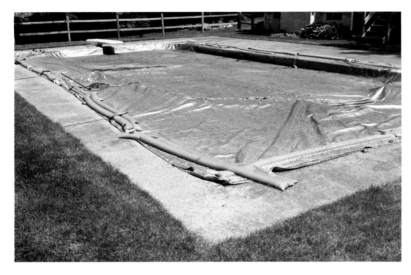

Solid covers keep out almost all winter debris, but they are unattractive and easily lift off the pool when water bags used to hold down the edges burst.
(Photo by Boyd Hagan; © TheTaunton Press, Inc.)

A mesh cover is secured with straps and bolts screwed into the pool surround. Some fine debris may filter through the mesh during the winter, but it is minimal.
(Photo by Judi Rutz; © The Taunton Press, Inc.)

Since my property is surrounded by woods, shade was a factor in the budgetary process. I discovered it would be necessary to take down several trees to have the pool in the sun. There were also half a dozen trees in the way, which had to be removed, stumps, roots, and all. There was no space to bury the stumps, so they had to be trucked away, an added expense for the machine time, trucking, and dumping.

VINYL-LINED VS. CONCRETE POOLS

The choice of a vinyl-lined versus a concrete pool is a major budgetary decision. I spoke with the real estate agent from whom

I purchased my home to learn about other pools in the neighborhood. I discovered that about half were vinyl-lined and half were concrete. I gleaned from the pool contractors that for just the pool alone, a vinyl-lined pool would cost between $15,000 and $18,000 and a concrete pool between $35,000 and $50,000. This estimate does not include fencing; landscaping; or electrical, lawn, or patio and deck work. And it may or may not include heating, lighting, extra stairs or ladders, or even water.

Between the base price and the extras, I figured on $30,000 for a vinyl-lined pool and $50,000 to $75,000 for a concrete pool. Since my house is worth less than $400,000, it was not hard to make the decision to go for a vinyl-lined pool. The neighborhood, the house value, and having six kids to put through college all contributed to that decision.

A vinyl-lined pool has forms made from fiberglass, plastic, steel, or concrete behind the liner. There are all sizes and many shapes from which to choose, but the shape and size must conform to the preset shapes of the forms: rectangular, oval, kidney, L-shaped, and several others, depending on the manufacturer. The liner lasts for about 10 years with normal use and comes in many designs and colors. There is a 3-ft. concrete pad around the top of the pool, which is an integral part of the structure. It can be augmented with more poured concrete, wooden decking, a dry-laid brick patio, concrete pavers, or natural stone; faced with flagstone or brick; colored; stamped with a pattern; or treated to keep it cool.

A concrete or gunnite pool can be any shape or size you want. The surface of the inside of the pool can be covered with a pebbly finish or left smooth and dyed in an array of colors. Colorful tiles are usually installed around the scum line. A 1-ft.-wide coping of concrete or stone is installed around the pool edge, and then you are free

to augment with a patio or wooden deck. The surface of the inside of the pool is expected to last for at least 25 years with routine maintenance.

POOL COVERS

Pool covers come in two forms: a solid plastic cover held in place by water bags and a nylon mesh cover, custom made to fit the shape of the pool and held in place by grommets inserted in the patio surface material. The solid plastic is about half the price of the mesh and is more effective in keeping leaves and debris out of the pool, but it is far less attractive, the water bags are not reliable, and it is not safe for people or animals to walk on the cover. Although I wouldn't walk on the nylon mesh cover, the manufacturer claims that it is possible to do so without sinking in.

PUMPS AND FILTERS

There are several pumps, filters, and heating systems from which to choose. Usually your contractor has a preference for which manufacturer's products he installs. He will recommend the size according to the size of the pool you choose and will also recom-

The pump, heater, and filter fit neatly on a 4-ft. by 6-ft. concrete base, easily disguised with fencing, plantings, or a pool house.
(Photo by Boyd Hagan; © The Taunton Press, Inc.)

Managing the Pool Project

With a realistic budget in place, you can work with your pool contractors by acting as project manager. This will ensure that the job comes together in a timely fashion. Your role as project manager is to keep track of everyone's schedule: arborist to take down trees, excavator, pool contractor, electrician, fencing contractor, and landscaper. Each phase of the project must be scheduled well in advance to keep the ball rolling. Keep a calendar to trigger a reminder call to each contractor as the one working on the current phase nears completion.

Be aware that weather is your worst enemy, and expect delays. Be patient and understanding if the workers are held up because of inclement weather, but ask for honest schedules and updates from the contractors all along the way.

Don't be afraid to ask questions and get involved throughout the process. Be there when the pool area is laid out to ensure that you are happy with the site. When you choose the site, remember to include the surrounding deck or patios, existing or to-be-built, so they will mesh with the design. The most important issue you must address if you are tying in existing decks or patios is the transition between those features and the new pool.

When my pool was completed, I was surprised to find that it was lower in the ground than I had expected. As a result, I had to build a low retaining wall and step down into the pool area, which I had not anticipated in the budget. The contractor had made a unilateral decision that the far end of the pool would be popped too far out of the ground and would need to be filled if he put the pool in at the height I wanted. Even though I was on site, there was a lack of communication. The lesson here: Be sure to not only be on hand but to speak up as well!

---

mend the type of filter: cartridge, sand, or DE (diatomaceous earth). Each has its advantages and disadvantages and its own price tag. The whole system can fit on a 4-ft. by 6-ft. concrete pad near the pool or be enclosed in a "pool house," which will add cost to the bottom line, depending on how elaborate you get.

FENCING

Fencing can run the gamut from tall solid stockade to the aluminum wrought-iron look to simple cedar post and rail. Some states and towns do not require fencing, but most do. And some can be very stringent about what is acceptable. My pool must have a 4-ft.-high fence with gate latches set at 54 in. That means the gateposts must be taller than the fencing. Because of my rural site, I have chosen three-rail cedar split-rail fencing covered with a vinyl-coated wire mesh, which must be attached to the fence on the side farthest from the pool, so that children cannot climb over the rails. I plan to grow vines on the wire to make it disappear. Of course, all this adds to the cost.

LANDSCAPING AROUND THE POOL

The decision of how elaborate to get with the landscaping is usually left for last. At the very least, you will want to repair lawn areas destroyed by the construction and the trucks and machinery. My minimal requirements were shrubs to hide the pump and filter units and vines to grow on the wire mesh. Since landscaping can be phased into a project, allow about $1,500 for repairs to the lawn and the immediate installation of a few shrubs and plan to do more the next year if the budget runs out.

Renovating a Pool

If you've inherited an old pool, you may experience one of two common problems: a hole or crack in the liner, or deterioration of the decking around the pool. Vinyl-lined pools require liner replacement when a hole or cracks appear. This can happen with age (the average liner life is 10 years) or by accident if something sharp pierces it. This is a serious problem that undermines the integrity of the pool, and the liner must be replaced by a pool contractor.

With both concrete and vinyl-lined pools, the patio or decking surrounding the pool may deteriorate either because of improper installation or the ravages of time. A mason or landscape contractor who is skilled in masonry can repair or replace patios, but seek the advice of a pool contractor before cutting away old concrete around a pool to make sure it is not an integral part of the pool structure. If it is part of the structure, you may choose to repair rather than replace it.

Bringing a Pond Back to Life

It is not unusual in rural areas to purchase property with a pond on it. Unfortunately, it is also not unusual for the pond to be overgrown and stagnant from neglect. Stagnation is usually caused by overgrowth. By cleaning up the edges and inside the pond itself, you should be able to bring it back to life. This presumes that there are underground springs feeding your pond and that it is not just seasonal water (there only after the snowmelt in the spring) or casual water (gathers after a storm because the ground is slow draining or consists of heavy clay underneath).

An elevated and cantilevered deck and walk enhance this small backyard pond, lush with plantings and protected from the neighbors by privacy fencing. (Photo © The Taunton Press, Inc.)

REMOVING TREES

You can do some of the work without the help of a machine, but it won't be easy. Select the trees and shrubs surrounding the pond that are worth keeping by first identifying them as you did the plants in your yard (see Chapter 2, beginning on p. 16). In this case, however, you have an additional factor to consider in the selection process: You must open up the pond to the sky, so that leaves from surrounding trees will not fall in the pond. The leaves produce methane gas as they break down, which fouls the pond. Also, algae grow in sun or shade, but thrive in oxygen-starved environments, which are typical of dank, dark, clogged up ponds.

So, in making your choices, look up as well as at ground level and remove trees that are blocking light. It is not important to remove stumps unless you want the banks to be pristine; in fact, removal of

The pond fits naturally into this setting, where the deck ties the house to its surroundings. (Photo by Charles Miller; © The Taunton Press, Inc.)

stumps and roots may cause the banks to become unstable.

REMOVING POND PLANTS

Next, you must attack the plants that have clogged the water. How you approach this depends on how bad it is clogged and how deep or large the pond is. If you can picture getting in a rowboat or donning some waders and yanking weeds by hand and with a rake, then the job is small and the pond is shallow. Most likely the weeds will be cattails and sedges, which can be removed with a shovel and mattock.

If the pond is large and deep, it may be necessary to drain it to perform this job effectively. If the pond was installed correctly, there should be a plug to pull to drain it. If not, you will need a machine to dig a dike, let the pond drain, scrape out the weeds, and install an overflow valve with a plug. Be sure to hire a skilled excavator who

knows how to build a pond. He may suggest that you reline the pond with heavy clay after the cleanup is done and before it is filled with water. By starting over in this fashion, you can be assured the water will be clean.

KEEPING THE WATER CLEAN

Once the weeds are removed and the pond has begun to fill again, the water should start to move again, which aerates it and keeps it clean. It may even be able to support fish, especially if you live in warmer climates where overwintering the fish is not a problem. They usually burrow into the mud of the banks of the pond to survive the winter, but in cool climates they must be tough fish, such as carp (goldfish).

You can also keep the water clean with oxygenating plants, such as *Myriophyllum* species, which release oxygen into the water and compete with algae for dissolved mineral salts. The oxygenators always win, and they keep the water clean. Some oxygenators are submerged, and some float on top of the water. Consult a water gardening catalog for ideas.

LANDSCAPING AROUND THE POND

Around the edges of the pond, you may want to install marginal and bog plants, which enjoy shallow water or transitional moist ground. Make sure you stick to plants that will not become weedy and start the overgrowth process all over again. There are many colorful plants in this category. They include certain irises (*Iris versicolor* and *I. sibirica*), arrowheads (*Sagittaria latifolia*), and many perennials. Hosta, lobelia, primroses, and astilbe all enjoy moist ground, and you can use dogwoods (*Cornus alba*), magnolia (*Magnolia virginiana*), and various willows (*Salix alba* and *S. matsudana* 'Tortuosa') for shrubby accents.

Of course, water lilies are what everyone pictures floating on a pond's surface, but beware. Unless they are planted in buckets, which will contain their rampantly spreading roots, and submerged, bucket and all, the pond will become clogged with the lilies. When the pond is drained for cleaning, you can build shelves out of soil to raise the buckets to the proper height (depending on the species, lilies should be submerged 12 in. to 36 in. below the surface) or place bricks or cement blocks on the bottom of the pond to place the buckets on. Tie a buoy or corked plastic bottle to the blocks to help locate them when the pond has filled with water.

Other potentially weedy but attractive plants, such as miniature cattails (*Typha minima*), sedges and rushes (*Juncus effusus spiralis*), and marsh marigolds (*Caltha palustris*), can be treated in the same way.

Siting a New Pond

If you're thinking of installing a pond, keep in mind that ponds are usually sited where there is water already, although this is not always the case. Water can be above ground or below ground. Aboveground standing water or surfacing springs make obvious targets as long as you are certain the water is not casual to the season (appears only after the snowmelt in spring, when the ground is still frozen underneath).

Nowadays, you also must be certain that you are not disturbing a wetland habitat, and you must seek permission to dig a pond near these areas. If you disturb a wetland without permission and are found out, you will be required to restore the wetland to its original character, which is a costly mistake. There are landscapers who deal exclusively in wetland restoration, and you should seek their advice.

One indicator of underground water is the plant material growing in an area. Some plants, such as arborvitae (*Thuja occidentalis*) and willows (*Salix* spp.), only grow naturally where there are underground springs. Dig where you find these plants, and there is sure to be water in the vicinity.

Although some feel it is far-fetched, water diviners (or witches as they are sometimes called) can detect underground water when their divining rods are tugged toward the ground. After receiving a diviner's advice, the presence of a few indicator plants would make me feel better before going to the expense of bringing in the backhoe, but I do believe there is something to this centuries-old method—I've seen it work more than once.

Try to choose an open site so that plenty of sun will hit the pond and falling leaves from trees won't clog it. Once you find the indicator plants, they can be removed to open up the site. In a sunny site, you'll be able to grow many water- and bog-loving plants. Make sure the site does not receive runoff from farmland and is not in a floodplain. Such areas can be contaminated by fertilizers and other chemical residues.

Creating a Water Feature

If a pond is too grand for your plan or if you don't have underground springs to support a pond, you can build a water feature in your yard. The goal is to have your small-scale man-made water feature look as natural as possible, so you'll need plants draping over the edges to soften the harsh lines and cover the edges of the plastic liner. When you picture a real pond or brook, you see meandering banks, edged with rocks and plants tucked into crevices. You can imitate Mother Nature by using the right plants and combining them with rocks.

How do you add a water feature to your yard? Start by installing a plastic preshaped pool. It's easy to install once you've dug a hole to accommodate the size and shape. You can customize your pool by using a heavy butyl rubber liner instead of the plastic—by doing so, you can make the pool any shape you want. Either way, you should be concerned about aerating the pool with a submerged pump, planting oxygenating plants, or introducing fish to keep the water clean. Fish need oxygen, but, in turn, they contribute to keeping the ecosystem in balance. They clean the pool by eating algae and other fouling agents.

Some plants, such as milfoils, actually help to oxygenate the water, which is critical for healthy fish. For this reason, it is best for the plants to become established before introducing the fish.

You can aerate a pool with a fountain to make it acceptable for fish. Big or small, a fountain will keep the water moving to establish a healthy environment. A fountain makes a tremendous focal point in a water feature and provides a pleasing symphony of sound. You can regulate the volume in most fountains to fit any preference, from gentle hum to raucous splash.

WATER PLANTS

Submerged water plants, such as water lilies, prefer quiet water and are prolific. They should be planted in containers, such as plastic pots, to keep their growth in check. Left to their own devices, they will quickly take over a pool or pond, choking out other plants and fouling the water by limiting sun and oxygen.

Water lilies are picky about water depth. Depending on the cultivar, water lilies thrive in depths from 12 in. to 36 in. You can accommodate their needs by building shelves at different levels beneath the water. You then plant the water lilies in the containers and place them on the shelves. Place the containers of young water lilies on bricks on the shelves and remove the bricks as the plants grow taller.

Water lilies prefer full sun, and there are several species—both hardy and tropical—to choose from. Most water lilies bloom during the day, but some tropicals flower at dusk and can be set off with dramatic lighting. Tropicals grow more quickly than the hardy cultivars and require a warm water temperature of at least 68°F. They must be removed from the outdoor garden and brought in to a heated greenhouse or conservatory water garden during the winter in temperate climates. Hardy water lilies should be planted in late spring or summer so they will be well established before winter arrives. They can remain in the pool over the winter and will burst forth with a vengeance the next growing season.

Certain iris varieties, marsh marigolds, and miniature cattails will grow in the water, too. In a small water feature, these plants, like water lilies, should be planted in rich compost and confined in barrels or crates to prevent them from clogging the pool. There are other floating plants that help shade the water for fish, provide food, and discourage algae growth. Get recommendations from a garden center that specializes in water features.

It is also a good idea to line the edges of the water with **moisture-loving perennials,** such as ferns, irises, grasses, and hostas. If you place the plants so that their foliage hangs over the edges and over rocks, it produces a lush, natural effect.

LANDSCAPING AROUND THE WATER FEATURE

To make the water feature look like a natural part of the environment, graduate the size of the plants as you move away from the

water to create a layered landscape that will blend with the rest of the yard. Moisture-loving shrubs are a good choice here, not only to enhance a wet area but also to attract wildlife with their colorful flowers and berries.

Although some leaf drop can't be helped, avoid siting a water feature where it will be inundated with leaves. A huge buildup of organic matter on the bottom of the pool will eventually foul the water with methane gas. You can put a cover over the water in the autumn and remove it in spring. Use a screen for a cover if you have fish overwintering in the water.

Adding Garden Structures

There are other features besides pools and ponds that can be added to your yard to make it more enjoyable, livable, and useful. For instance, garden structures, such as gazebos and other shade structures, can be a relaxing escape. They should be carefully

Tropical plants enjoy the humid atmosphere surrounding this water feature. Water lilies, planted in buckets and submerged in the water, stay in check. (Photo courtesy *Fine Gardening* magazine; © The Taunton Press, Inc.)

placed in the yard to take advantage of views and quiet spaces.

I prefer a garden house like a gazebo or a shade structure to be "far from the madding crowd." They are great places to which to retreat to read or enjoy a good snooze. If you feel the same way, choose a site accessible to the house (handy when you need a drink) but far enough away to be out of the line of fire of play spaces and work areas. Even a hammock strung between trees is a great escape.

Structures in work areas, which include sheds, cold frames, and compost heaps, need prudent siting as well. They generally are placed near gardens, garages, or other existing outbuildings and, because they aren't usually the beauty spots of the yard, should be placed so they are not focal points.

Planning Play Areas

For quick and easy access to a play space, the best location is close to a door of the house and near windows so you can check on your children. If the area is enclosed by fencing, make the space large enough for active play and install the fence posts without concrete, so that the fence can be removed later when the kids are grown.

Shade is an important consideration in a play area, especially if there is a sandbox, which absorbs heat. If there are no trees to provide shade for at least part of the space, you should construct a shade structure. Even large beach umbrellas or a freestanding arbor with canvas stretched over it will be helpful.

An older child's open play space replete with swing set, slide, and other built-in toys still should be accessible to the house and

A rustic arbor sits quietly amid the landscape, tucked into the woods for shade and privacy. (Photo by Delilah Smittle; © The Taunton Press, Inc.)

shade. Wood and metal equipment also absorb heat, so shade is a must.

Siting a Vegetable Garden

Some homeowners enjoy tending—and harvesting—a vegetable garden. Whatever size vegetable garden you make, it must be sited in the sun for best production. Stay away from trees that drop leaves; decomposing leaves rob nitrogen from the soil while they break down, and they can spread diseases that affect the garden.

Make sure the site is protected from wind because pollination will be affected by excessive wind. If wind is a problem for your garden, build a fence or other permeable barrier to baffle and minimize the breeze or plant a windbreak of evergreen trees and shrubs near the intended garden site. A solid barrier is not advisable because it tunnels wind and actually increases the wind's velocity as it goes over or under the barrier.

The garden should be accessible to water, so don't site it farther than your hose can reach. You may need to put up fencing to protect the garden from animals. Some people even resort to electric fencing; if you think you might, be sure to site your garden near an electrical source.

START SMALL

I always recommend starting small with a vegetable garden because the upkeep can be overwhelming. You can always add to it next year. A 12-ft. by 15-ft. plot will provide a lot of vegetables as long as you plan it well. Plant in beds small enough to reach into it from all sides without walking in—it's more efficient than planting in rows. Create pathways between the beds for easy access.

Grow vining vegetables on trellises or poles to create more space, and interplant

The bed system of planting a vegetable garden allows easy access from all sides for maintenance and harvesting. It also creates a mosaic of textures and colors, making the vegetable garden a beautiful landscape as well. (Photo by Judi Rutz; © The Taunton Press, Inc.)

vegetables. Interplanting—mixing fast-growing crops like radishes or lettuce with slower growers like cabbage and turnips—is useful for maximizing space and keeping pests away from a susceptible crop like tomatoes. Strong-smelling and -tasting crops like mint and garlic or flowers like marigolds are good companions for tomatoes because they repel pests.

Be sure to plant tall vegetables, such as corn, or trellised vegetables, such as cucumbers, beans, or squash, in the northern end of the garden so they will not shade other, lower-growing vegetables.

Lighting the Landscape

Good lighting can enhance any landscape, but it is especially useful for updating an existing landscape. You can easily install low-voltage lighting on your own after a licensed electrician connects the 120-voltage line from the house to a transformer. Low-voltage lighting is excellent for landscapes and task lighting because of its versatility, easy installation, and comparatively

Updating the landscape with lighting is a simple and inexpensive way to renovate. Here a winter landscape is enhanced by proper lighting. (Photo courtesy Nightscaping.)

Task lighting should be at your feet where the light is needed. Fixtures for task lighting are more ornamental than other low-voltage lights because they are meant to be seen. (Photo courtesy Nightscaping.)

inexpensive fixtures. Many modern-day fixtures are designed to feature the light they shed, not the fixture itself. Most of these fixtures are black or green rust-free aluminum, to blend in with the surrounding landscape.

The myth that low-voltage lighting is not a strong enough light source is untrue. As long as it is installed correctly, using only 80 percent of the total voltage indicated for a strand of fixtures with the proper wattage of bulbs, there will be no voltage drop or dimness at the end of the strand. Many lines can be drawn from the transformer (dependent on its size), and many lights can be attached to one line, following the 80 percent rule.

The transformer can be buried in the ground in a watertight box, hidden behind a shrub, or put in a garage or shed. The lines emanating from it can be buried just under the soil or under mulch in a planting bed. The fixtures usually are attached to stakes, allowing great flexibility in how they may be spaced as long as enough slack is left in the line. This also allows you to move the fixture as a plant grows larger or if you later add plants to a bed.

LIGHTING OPTIONS

There are four ways to light the landscape: uplighting, backlighting, downlighting, and task lighting. Fixtures for uplighting are spiked into the ground and placed at the base of trees and shrubs for effect.

Backlighting fixtures are spiked into the ground in front of an interesting-shaped tree, shrub, or bed of perennials or ferns. This focuses light on the specimens and creates a shadow on the wall behind them. Downlighting fixtures are hung in trees to highlight interesting branching habits.

Task lighting should be at your feet where the light is needed. There are many low-voltage lamps for pathway lighting, and

they are usually more ornamental than the fixtures used to light up the landscape. These fixtures are meant to be seen—rather than hiding the fixtures under trees or shrubs, make them focal points.

All outdoor lighting should be carefully placed so that it doesn't shine directly into your eyes. You also should avoid overdoing it. A great amount of lights may be right for a restaurant or parking lot, but around your home, subtlety is key, which is why low-voltage lighting is so effective.

Finishing Touches

It is the finishing touches that make your gardens unique, reflecting your personality and stamping your hallmark on all your hard work. The most fun part of gardening for me is adding ornament and whimsy to planting beds, patios, and decks. Container gardens, filled with small trees, flowers, or vegetables, are one way to do this. Sculpture, whether as a focal point or tucked away in quiet recesses, is another. Naturally placed rocks add visual impact to the landscape. Even

your choice of garden furniture gives your yard a personalized look.

CONTAINER GARDENS
Container gardens house various contents—flowers, herbs, vegetables, even small trees—and the containers are just as diverse. Garden centers have an array of bunnies, frogs, and gazing balls, but I've been planting with wire mesh forms. I line them with sphagnum moss, fill them with soil, and plant colorful dwarf snapdragons, verbena, lobelia, and variegated ivy in them.

Moss-lined wire mesh planters make whimsical accents in the garden or on the deck or patio. (Photo by Boyd Hagan; © The Taunton Press, Inc.)

Container vegetable gardens are perfect for small spaces. Use trellises to accommodate vining veggies like cucumbers and squash. (Photo by Boyd Hagan; © The Taunton Press, Inc.)

One is shaped like a watering can, and it hangs by its handle in pouring position. Another is a cup-and-saucer shape filled with alyssum and creeping thyme. And the most whimsical of all are the pair of high-heeled slippers I filled with miniature hens and chicks. Container gardens that reflect your individuality add the finishing touch to your renovated deck, patio, or front stoop.

Regardless of what you plant in containers—annuals, trees and shrubs, herbs, or vegetables—the key to successful planting is using well-drained, sterile soil mixed with plenty of organic matter and watering diligently to prevent the containers from drying out.

GARDEN FURNITURE

Garden furniture can be found in any mail-order gardening catalog and at home centers, but some interesting pieces are made from rocks and logs left from the excavation of the pool or renovation of the woods.

You can make a rustic, but serviceable, bench for a woodland setting with two flat-topped rocks and a log. Cut the log in half lengthwise for the bench seat and make a notch on the bottom (the rounded side) for the rocks. Set the rocks in place (these are the bench legs) and lay the log on top of the two rocks. This bench also looks nice amidst the flowers in a perennial border.

You might be able to find a long, flat rock for the seat instead of a log. Either way, the beauty of this kind of furniture is that there is no need to worry about painting or preserving it, and it fits the landscape perfectly.

SCULPTURE

Sculpture can add visual interest to a landscape. Placed at the center of the garden, sculpture becomes a focal point. Many formal gardens are built around a figurine or fountain. A birdbath makes a good center focal point as well. Sculpture can also be used more subtly. I prefer sculpture or ornaments tucked away in nooks and crannies next to rocks, beneath shrubs, or in any unlikely place a visitor will find delight in when happening upon it. You can cover the bases or pedestals of ornaments by using plants with graceful, drooping leaves (such as daylilies, hosta, or ferns).

ROCKS IN THE GARDEN

If your yard is anything like mine, you have an abundance of boulders, which, in my case, came out of the ground with the excavation of the pool and the subsequent blasting of its bottom. The trick to using rocks in the landscape is to make them look as naturally placed as possible. This requires imagination and resistance to the tendency to just line them up. For a focal point in a garden, you want the rocks to look like the

A rustic bench fashioned out of old wooden planks and stumps fits perfectly into an informal woodland scheme. (Photo by Lee Anne White; © The Taunton Press, Inc.)

Flat rocks were used to form this very natural looking stone bench. (Photo by Ken Druse.)

glacier deposited them there millions of years ago.

Artful placement is usually accomplished with an odd number of rocks of different sizes and shapes, but of the same geological type. Use them as a backdrop for the garden or with smaller rocks for a few plants. If the rocks have moss or lichens growing on them, even better. Dig in rocks by burying about a quarter of each rock in the ground to make it look "planted."

Arrange plants and shrubs around the rocks, heeding the plants' potential for growth. You don't want to cover up the rocks, so use plants that stay in proportion at maturity—these add to the notion of the rocks having been there forever. Good plant choices are alpine perennials (perennials that grow no taller than 1 ft.), dwarf conifers (very slow-growing evergreens), and ground-hugging creeping plants. These should be planted in layers, not in a ring around the rocks.

Rock garden plantings include perennials, alpine perennials, and dwarf conifers. Rocks are arranged to resemble natural looking outcroppings. (Photo by Susan Roth.)

If you don't already have a ledge to create the garden in, arrange the rocks so they look like outcroppings of the same ledge. The rocks should be turned the same way and should rise intermittently out of the ground, usually down a slope.

Index